Qliphoth

Flesh Totems & Bone Masks, Opus 2

Arranged by

EDGAR KERVAL

Edited by

TIMOTHY

✦ **BECOME A LIVING GOD**

COPYRIGHT

ORDERS

View a complete catalog at: BecomeALivingGod.com.

DISCLAIMER

CREDITS

Authors: Andrew Dixon, R.N. Lant, S. Ben Qayin, Kyle Fite, Angela Edwards, Alexei Dzyuba, Claudio Cesar De Carvalho, Sean Woodward

Editor: Edgar Kerval

Editor: Timothy Donaghue

Publisher: Become A Living God ✶

Sands of Time

Though the sands of time,
And evocation primal forces,
Rises from hidden portals,
A gnosis showing us the path.
It enlightens us with ineffable light,
And brings transcendence with its primigenian wisdom.

The scales of the Black Serpent are open,
To show forbidden, poisonous dreams.
Drink this sacred elixir,
Travel beyond time and space.

We are all and none.
We are all the void,
That resides in Qliphothic energies.
Through flesh totems and mask bones,
We rise.

EDGAR KERVAL
Colombia ✦

Tablet of Qliphoth

Ralifu

𝕿𝖍𝖊 𝕸𝖆𝖌𝖎𝖈𝖎𝖆𝖓 𝕬𝖘 𝖁𝖆𝖒𝖕𝖎𝖗𝖊

Andrew Dixon

THE magician, in the guise of shaman, witch, magus or siddha, is a mover or manipulator of the energies used in many forms to perform acts of magick, either by integrating herself to channels of force in order to focus or direct this energy onto the arena of hir will. Raising power through the use of ritual in ceremonial magic, calling on the forces of nature as a witch. In lodges and covens or as a lone practitioners using pranayama, tantric or kundalini yogic techniques – directing thought-forms and familiars, spirits, daemons and elementals to perform acts on hir behalf. By altering hir own mental state (using meditative or chemical means) energy is used and released. It being the application or rather the focus/deployment of the kundalini/prana/ki/orgone energy which is essential to the workings of the magical operation.

Throughout the world various Religio-magical cultures use or have used practices which could be considered vampiric. Aztecs, Babylonians and Greeks used blood sacrifice to attract the attention of the gods and daemons, the belief being that from the emanations of the blood, discarnate entities could take on form to make themselves visible or even material on the human plane of existence. The Catholics consumption of the wafer and the wine, the body and the blood of Christ.

The Thelemites Liber XLIV, the Mass of the Phoenix (although in this case the consumption is more than symbolic). The Jivaro Indians of Ecuador who after killing their enemies, take the heads and following an established ritual, remove the skull and shrink the head-skin to the size of a fist.

These shrunken-heads (tsantsa) are used in a variety of magical rites or "Alternatively, pure power can be drawn from the tsantsa using a form of vampirism in which the muisak [the avenging, second soul in the Jivaro belief system] can be made to re-enter the tsantsa in order for it to draw in itskakarma; [power] this is said to increase fertility. Interestingly, the vampire bat is an image of the muisak, connecting the concept of power accumulation with blood and death."1 These as many other, magical systems are generally available for the cost of a paperback book. This essay is directed towards the use of various practices by the vampire- magician in the acquisition of energies for the use in ritual using methods typically frowned upon as vampiric in nature. The vampire being a creature who steals or charms the blood/energy from another for hir own use. The moral ambiguities of these acts are, of course, left to the individual practitioner.

𝕰theric 𝕱eeding

The fact of psychic vampirism is well known in most systems of magic, the vampire being a person who unknowingly or intentionally draws from the life-force of those around hir – either to sustain themselves or, in some instances, to subjugate them, to have them submit to their will. It is this auric energy or life-force which these individuals siphon off from their victims, causing lethargy and/or reducing their natural resistance (both physical and spiritual). Any competent magician who is proficient in the visualization and directing of energies can use this if desired to perform acts of vampirism. Drawing in of ki from others is possible by the positive perception and manipulation of ones own energy field to assess and retain these forces. The proximity of person/s of outgoing natures with high energy levels for this form of absorption is obviously required, these should be people who will easily

Restore their own energy without undue physical or mental stress, of which a little will be said at a later point. While drawing the auric energy of others can empower one providing extra power for the individual it is the subtler emanations that are of more use to the vampire magician to replenish hir own extended or added to hir own to empower ritual. Sexual techniques used by many magical groups or individuals are no longer "occult" in the true sense of the word and the use of these by a magician would forgo the need of any so called vampiric method as it is the creation/exchange of the vibrations originated by these acts which are used to vitalize the ritual enacted. The following techniques are the sole province of the vampire-magician who working alone wishes to access these energies for hir own use.

Astral Rape – Succubi & Incubi

The earliest known representation of a vampire shows her in the act of copulation with a man and we have just observed that Weyer regards the Hebrew Lilith as queen of the succubi.2

Sexual energies are some of the most potent forms extant – the nature of the sexual act, as much of the intention, determining the tone of the vibrations released – those being used to access the levels required to execute varying rituals and operations. The magician can make use of a VIII° (masturbatory) working hirself to obtain the sexual energies of another to empower a ritual with the required vitality.

Using whichever forms of sigilisation, solipsism or sympathetic magic endemic to the magician's belief system, a link to the object of hirs attentions and the specifics of the type of working should be fabricated as required. Then while at the point of exhaustion or sleep s/he should fixate on the sigil or link while at the same time stimulate hirself to the point of orgasm, stopping as near as possible before the point of climax is reached.

This form of karezza should be continued, without release, until sleep occurs. At this point the subconscious (form) of the practitioner will seek release and directed by whatever link is being used will focus on the object of desire on the astral to enact the form of congress specified in the ritual in the form of an incubi or succubi assault on the vampire-magician's victim. The energy or vibrations released can then be used to perform the chosen working or returned to the magician for absorption by hirself or into the prepared sigil which can then be used as the focus for a later working. This can be of particular use to those needing access to the lunar energies discharged during the dark phase of the moon cycle, which, due to the irnature can be problematic to secure.

Any form of sexual release will in many instances attract other entities, some of which by the nature of the act will be vampiric. Care then should be taken to protect the incubi/succubi form of the magician. One of the most potent defences available is the assumption of the god-from Hoor-Parr-Kraat (Harpocrates) in the shape of "an egg of vivid blue light flocked with gold;

like a stainless summer sky shot through with beams of sunlight. Sexual vampires, seeing this radiant wall of light are drawn precipitately towards it and dash themselves to pieces."3

This (and many others) is a construct which will both protect the vampire's astral form and act as a vessel to contain the relevant odic vibrations. The reader should realize that approaching anyone using magical forms as described or wards to block or deflect attacks should be avoided, any form of duel or combat on these levels will result in a loss of energies on both sides leaving each participant open to further assault while weakened. It is for the same reasons that one should consider carefully the choice of target in any

Vampiric attack. Someone who naturally has a high level of whichever form of energy desired will be able to replenish themselves easily given a sufficient interval. Constant assaults on any individual will create a deficiency in that person making them unsuitable as a donor not only due to their low levels of energy but also that due to their situation the victim will seek to, even unconsciously, restore that which has been taken from them. Latching onto the assailant or even onto others around them, thus creating another psychic vampire who without the control of the vampire-magician will continue to feed unchecked and uncontrolled.

It is in the form of unfulfilled sexual obsessions that many unintentional vampires, succubi and incubi and engendered. Books containing examples of such entities abound, the works dealing with the Magus Daskalos provide several contemporary examples. One of these describes the shade of a young man who dies of tuberculosis after having been engaged for four years without having intercourse with his fiancée. "He died with this unfulfilled craving. This overwhelming yearning for her kept him floating in the etheric world from where he began harassing her. The girl was going mad.

Each night before she would go to bed he would semi-hypnotize her and induce her to keep the window of her room open. He would then enter inside as a bat and would come to her. The bat would wedge on her neck and draw blood and etheric."4

Familiars

The use of a familiar or servitor by a vampire-magician is fundamentally the same as that used by any other magical practitioner and can be an effective technique in either providing sustenance from the absorption of life-force or auric energy or the specific essences taken from drinking of the chakra lotuses. A familiar (whether natural, called forth or created) to be used by the magician as a stealer of energies should be by its nature a predatory creature. If for nothing more than the sake of tradition bats, wolves and cats are ideal choices. The entity or form of said creatures predisposes it to its task, that of being sent on the behest of its creator to pilfer energies to be returned for absorption by the magician. The advantage of the use of a familiar in this way means that its owner can, if having given the familiar a degree of autonomy let it continue to seek out and replenish its master with energy until it is stopped or is recalled to perform other tasks.

The individuals own input in the conception and use of these entities as well as the care taken in their maintenance is that which will determine the effectiveness of the use of such familiars. Unfortunately they will of course lack the innate sensibilities and awareness of the sender, so special care should be taken in both the instructing of the familiar in the task, as well as the harvesting of such energies that are obtained in this fashion. Otherwise the magician could find hirself poisoned by the very nourishment s/he has sought.

Chakra Drinking

Other than the natural auric energy given off by people and the vibrations released by various methods of sexual magic, specific vibrations/powers are also intimately linked to the chakra points of the body. These sites are the subject of much study and many books have been written on the methods of empowering and accessing the chakras.

They should be studied in detail before embarking on any process involving raising or raiding the perfumes of these flowers either individually or in sequence as in the arousing of the Kundalini Serpent. The study of these centres will indicate to the adherent the dangers which are involved in any assault of this persuasion as the unbalancing of these vortices can result in the disruption or even degeneration of the psyche in both the vampire and the victim.

Those who are aware of the hazards associated with attempting to vampirically procure such energies can use either hir familiars directed by hir will or by projecting hirself astrally using whatever methods their magical paradigm involves. Otherwise direct contact would be required and necessitate a potentially willing participant in the vampire-magician's rites where the bringing forth of diverse energies can be accomplished by the laying on of hands, drawing in via breath or through the eyes dependent on the facility of the individual.

While as mentioned, assiduous study of all the chakras is essential it is perhaps worth referring briefly to the chakra which is located at the most beloved point to all vampires, the throat. The locus being known variously as the Visuddha-chakra, Akasa and Daath. Many authorities have written concerning the development and use of the vibrations emanating from this point, Sir John Woodroffe states, referring to the Visuddha-chakra "He sees the three periods,* [*Past, present and future – Note by J.W.] and becomes the benefactor of all, free from disease and sorrow and long-lived." 5 While from Kenneth Grant "The symbolism of the serpent drinking fluid which flows from the higher lotuses, especially in the region of the Visuddha (throat) chakra could easily be misinterpreted as a formula of vampirism, and the

Origin of the vampire legend may well have its roots in this tantric-yogic process. The nectar of Immortality is the soma, or Moon Juice."6 Being the locale of Daath (death) this point is the entrance to Universe-B or the Tunnels of Set in Kenneth Grant's "Nightside of Eden", the plane of the qliphoth, some of whom it is said are merely shells of once living persons, ghouls, revenants and elementals who exist only by vampirising the living of their vitality. It is for this reason that magicians are warned against having commerce with such entities and why the vampire- magician does. For in venturing into the arena of vampirism one is positioning oneself at a very definite point in the magical food chain. Any other vampiric entity therefore can be defined as your hunter, competition or food.

Vampiric Entities

As has been described in this discourse there are a variety of entities that are vampiric in nature. From unintentionally or consciously created thought-forms to shades of the dead and the human psychic vampire all can pose a degree of threat (dependent on their own skills and abilities) to the vampire-magician, but also open up new realms of possibilities.

A psychic-vampire will already be drawing energy from others and consequently will make an ideal quarry, their energy system also being inclined to the flow of vitality making the draining of life-force more accessible. The normal bias of the psychic vampire's system is to the absorption of energy, care therefore is called for so as not to enter into a "tug-of-war" engagement. Safeguarding one's own position by assuming god forms or performing the Rose Cross Ritual for self-enclosure and protection of the astral body.

Spirits and/or shades can be invoked using ceremonial techniques and then bound to the magician's will as a familiar, using a potentially riskier approach involving shamanistic, dervish or voodoo practices, the shade can be allowed to possess the devotee in order to impart its vitality or pass on knowledge or abilities to the adept.

The major risk being that if the entity is stronger than the magician rather than assimilating the creature as intended, s/he will then become the victim. Alternatively, "spirit traps" can be fashioned from especially prepared crystals, boxes or even rooms can be contrived to ensnare thought-forms or creatures on the astral. Once captured these can be restrained and dealt with at the magician's leisure in whatever manner s/he deems suitable or requires.

Another approach to acquiring vampiric endowments involves the accessing of the 18th Tunnel of Set, ascribed to The Chariot on the Tree of Life and tarot, this tunnels sentinel is Characinth. From Aleister Crowley's comments on this path in Liber CCXXXI "He rideth upon the chariot of eternity."7 The forms of energy (kalas) associated with this tunnel yield the ability to cast enchantments, the capability to assuage ones needs and attain magical immortality. The danger being the addiction to those same energies which will then destroy the magician from depletion through hir relentless pursuit of the substances, that s/he believes will sustain hir, to the exclusion of everything else.

Other tunnels which may be of particular interest to the vampire- magician include that of Niantiel, the 24th tunnel (Death in the dayside tarot) whose Plutonian energies revel in transformations. Parfaxitas, the 27th tunnel beneath the Tower, the sexual formula of which (VIII°+) deals with the assuming of animal forms on the astral. Or even the 29th tunnel of Qulielfi. This tunnel, being the dark side of The Moon holds the keys to dealing with energies on many subtle levels and existing as it does in twilight, the in-between areas of life/death, sleep and waking make it a sublime arena for the workings of any magick.

While only giving an overview of several concepts on the use of magical vampiric techniques rather than detailed descriptions of rituals and practices (any of which can be developed or deduced by any able practitioner) it is hoped that the reader will realize that this short treatise is not a guide or recommendation on magical practice. The descriptions and examples of some of these acts providing sufficient warning of the dangers likely to afflict the follower of such a system and hir victims. ✦

Bibliography

1 Stephen Sennitt: *Monstrous Cults*, p 36-37.
2 Montague Summers: *The Vampire His Kith and Kin*, p. 228-9.
3 Kenneth Grant: *Cult of the Shadow*, p. 178-179.

4 Kyriacos C. Markides: *The Magus of Strovolos*, p. 161.

5 Sir John Woodroffe: *The Serpent Power*, p. 390.

6 Kenneth Grant, *The Magical Revival*, p.148.

7 Aleister Crowley: *Gems from the Equinox*, p. 667.

The Tellum

Scorpionis

R.N. Lant

One Magic

Understood that our Earth exist due to balance only. Our planet turns on its own axis. If the balance vanishes, the earth will collapse and disappear.

I understood its similarity with us. We need balance or we will collapse and disappear as well. The balance factor is to stay realistic...

T O believe in the hidden world, the truth other than the one which was imposed became something more allowable for the persons gifted with time, secret, reliable relations and clear tolerance (categorized as intolerance by the common fool in most of the cases). After all, it is not one of the first steps towards wisdom there is to realize that perhaps one can overtakes possibilities on the « not possible.

In a comprehensible vision of occultism, one must remain humble in front of the universal knowledge and the studies of the left hand path & the right hand path, as one can't possibly go without the other if one wants to achieve greatness within the dark arts. The magick. There is no magic reserved for this or that culture, religion or cult, many essences, many different names but one single magick. The fundamental aspect of its practices is simply universal; a single force, a single magic, a whole - one who governs, under the veil, the natural equilibrium of things. As logic teaches us, without hate there is not love, without sadness there is no step in joy, and the essences of these Ying-Yang's are reaching another level of power when achieved side by side with their opposite pairs.

The same principle takes there in relation as regards this logical suite: without the invisible, there is just no visible. Perhaps a sentence which might bring some confusion within minds but all shall be clear and limpid as clear spring water in its own time but by looking at it well, is it so unlikely? Forces or power is therefore a universal thing, through the visible as by the invisible. As every culture aimed to develop certain, dark branches of arts in these different doctrines, others were bare exclusively by the Mesopotamians by example. The Middle East has always been exposed in a powerful sphere, where energies cross and where the people evolved in a more advanced manner than others, but still is accessible to any magus of a certain respected level or wisdom.

Gnostic Dualism: Ingressus Scorpionis

Traditionally the Scorpion has been associated with male sexuality, destruction, the occult, the mystical, illumination, healing and resurrection. Centuries ago, the Scorpion was the agent of divine vengeance. The Scorpion in this context was regarded as the instrument of divine vengeance in itself.

In Babylon, Orion, the Hunter is the heavenly representation of the earthly Nimrod, known for his might within the art of hunting down his enemies and the tower of Babel. The name of a Scorpion in Chaldee (ancient Semitic people who ruled in Babylonia) is Akrab, but Ak-rab, thus divided, signifies 'The Great Oppressor' and this is the hidden meaning of the Scorpion as represented in the Zodiac. That sign typifies him who cut off the Babylonian god, and suppressed the rules and system which were putted in place. Also, in Egypt, it was while the Sun was in the House of Scorpio that Osiris 'disappeared' and great lamentations were made for his disappearance, thus making him an agent of the Red Lord Set.

The Scorpio is as well the symbolic of the occult initiation to the darkest arts, the one who leads to knowledge and embraces Darkness in its whole. A powerful symbolic which advocates equilibrium in all matters, and which is considered as one of the fundamental philosophies of Traditional Satanism and from the ancient philosophies of the cult of Seth (Some of these can still be seen today within the tomb of the Pharaoh Setnakhte (20th Dynasty) in the Valley of the Kings. You understand there that once again, may you take a side or the other, may you be an adept of the Left Hand Path or its counter-part, the two opposites are inexorably attracted, and sometimes unite to and towards each other, one cannot survive without the other. Seth as the sworn enemy of his brother Osiris, still join his force to maintain a certain equilibrium within the darkness and vice-versa, same goes for the other side, and it is as such that only powerful studies and practices of the Occult are possible, one cannot learn mighty skills without knowing how the other side works as well! It is in this form of thoughts that Gnosticism was born; out of the darkness.

Gnosticism (a synthesis of occultism and Jewish Christianism) was a brutal heretic philosophy which started in Alexandria, Egypt and constituted a great threat to the early Holy Church. During the Middle Ages, the Inquisition was directed largely at Gnostic sects such as the Templars, Cathars, Albigenses, Bogomils and the Donatists. Although these groups were eradicated by the Church of Rome, the secret doctrine which they represented was carried forward by a myriad of secret societies spawned by the Invisible College of the Order of the Rosy Cross during the 17th century Rosicrucian Enlightenment. In the middle ages, The Inquisition realized that Gnostic covens were constituted mainly of people who belonged to prestigious orders such as the Templars, Katharian warlords, Albigeans, Bogomils and Donatists. Even if those groups were eradicated by the Vatican, their secret doctrines were reported and passed through generations after generations, some kept in safety and away from the most dedicated followers of the Left Hand Path by l' Ordre de la Croix Rosy in the 17th century which is better known these days under the name of the Rosicrucian Order.

This battle against the Christian Doctrine is actually based upon facts and logics based upon universal dualism: two forces opposing each other on an equal level on a continual struggle to believe on one side that there is a almighty divine figure who created the Universe and its opposite Demiurge, which is a true emanation of a pure essence who created the physical earth which is in itself an Infernal dwelling place. Whilst dualistic Gnostics believe that matter is evil and Spirit is good, monistic Gnostics regard matter not as evil, but as an illusion.

"To believe in God, you need faith, to believe in the devil, you just have to open your Eyes..." Something to think about! My speech might sound chaotic and maybe a bit monotonous to some for now, but one is to be teach how to read in between the lines if he wants to achieve greatness within the Dark Arts and learn to see what lies on the other side of his own face. All shall be cleared to the ones who find the keys and unlock their own sight!

Regarding Blavatsky, the fall of the astral being Adam Kadmon (primal man) led to a drastic transformation within the spiritual belief of the ancient world and made obsolete its actual material situation. The cataclysm related to the first fall was taken in consideration by the followers of the Right Hand Path by an alteration within the sign of Virgo–Scorpio:

Virgo the pure is separated, and from the decreasing of generations, or decreasing of cycles, becomes Scorpio symbol of Sin and matter."(209:502 s.) Scorpio, however, states Fred Getting in The Secret Zodiac, still retains a dual image—the eagle and scorpion—a duality which represents the two natures of man:

Apparently because of its primordial role as the consort of Virgo, the Great Mother Goddess and archetype before Isis, the astrological sign of Scorpio will preside over the restoration of mankind to its previous spiritual state. In reason of her primordial role as the consort of Virgo, the Great Divine Mother Isis, the sign of Scorpio will prevail and will preside at the unanimous symbolic of the restoration of humanity in its original and instinctive state of Spirituality, the agent of men's true nature in this matter, far from the blind folds and brain washings the world knows today since the 19th century.

Worldwide occult source agree on the point that a transformation a step back on the matter through the «whole world» will occur within the house of the Scorpio.

From early scrolls and tablets to our contemporary discoveries in the matter (and I am not talking here about your usual kind of "Occultism for Dummies" books and other unreliable works of this kind) this has been a proved factor by the people of experience within the practices of the dark Arts and Secret Knowledge. Think about it, after all it is just pure logic... One cannot reach the Angelic Realm, may it be with his fists or his behind without knowing the corridors leading to the "Pearly Gates of Heaven". It is always the one who spreads the greatest light who cast the darkest shadow upon the unenlightened and is therefore considered as the bringer of darkness...

Oordo ab Chao

I absolutely not pretend to be the agent of THE truth, there are many truths to be seen and understood, as the ones who confine themselves within their own vision without expending the inadmissible, dwell within a hollow world. Fact is that the light of darkness has proven time and time again that its light shines brighter than the supposedly righteous path engendered by Yahweh and his cohorts. No need here to quote again this or that as we all know that this is just facts and therefore shall be used to reach the ascent every practitioner is in reach of. Now it is up to the adept to forge his own weapons, build his own path and walk his way upon the path of the worth or fall on his face that very time too much and be swiped aside as he cannot learn his lesson. The path of darkness is a dangerous road but oh so beautiful for the ones who walk their journey through with humbleness and wisdom, through the Qliphoth and across the bridge of Da'at and Bar Shasketh. These being just listed as example of course (always better to clarify for those stupid enough to even try or think they can try reaching these before reaching a minimum of understanding), no order comes without chaos and no understanding without confusion, the secret Knowledge has been kept this way for centuries and for very good reasons and since the last years there is a recrudescence of interests within the matter compared to the last two centuries... is it due to some awakening? Hollywood?

The occult Black Metal scene or something else? The only thing that is important is that we don't care, we shouldn't care as only our own path is what matters, are we going to deal with it with haste or with wisdom and balance? Are you gonna be the dove, the vulture or the scorpion? Confusion has always been the key to understanding, the root of all knowledge and the treasure chest waiting to be open by the one, unique key.

This article may seem insignificant or even boring to some but how do you think of those keys were kept away from the eyes of the unworthy during the last millennia? ✦

by kazim

The Arte of Blood

S. Ben Qayin

BLOOD... glorious elixir of life, that which brings light to the darkened eyes of lone night shades, giving breath again to those who dwell in shadow light. It is the fiery essence of magic run course through your burning veins, and the strength of the consuming spirits that drink in its power, whoever wander the halls of endless mists. Blood has an energy to it that many react to; there is something inherently 'forbidden', or sacred that we feel when experiencing it. It is our essence, the spirit liquefied and warm...it is Alchemical, as both a material and a spiritual essence combined into one ever changing beautiful form which gives life and possess power... it is existence.

Much has been written of blood in connection with the spiritual. It has drawn our attention as a race, and been woven into our sacred and holy rites throughout history, imbedded within both philosophic and theological thought, as well as in ritual praxis as central religious applications and symbology. In the Christian bible their god is quoted as saying if one drinks of it, they shall be 'cut off' from heaven and salvation:

> For it is the life of all flesh; the blood of it is for the life thereof: therefore I said to the children of Israel, You

shall eat the blood of no manner of flesh: for the life of all
flesh is the blood thereof: whoever eats it shall be cut off.

—Leviticus 17:14, American King James Version

And yet within their very own rites of Eucharist, they drink
wine which is magically/alchemically transformed into the
blood of their savior, which makes for an interesting contradic-
tion to the previous passage considering Jesus' own words, Regardless, it is seen by Christians as something sacred

He who eats My flesh and drinks My blood has eternal
life, and I will raise him up on the last day. For My flesh
is true food, and My blood is true drink. He who eats my
flesh, and drinks my blood, dwells in me, and I in him.

—John 6:54, King James Version

That either belongs only to their god, or that can only be consumed by followers from the veins of the son of their God, Jesus
Christ. Holy blood is also a reoccurring theme in the phenomena
known as 'Stigmata', which occurs to believers of Christ who
wish to feel his sacrifice and pain. Often the supernatural scene
is filled with sacred blood.

All of a sudden there was a dazzling light. It was as
though the heavens were exploding and splashing forth
all their glory in millions of waterfalls of colors and stars.
And in the center of that bright whirlpool was a core of
blinding light that flashed down from the depths of the
sky with terrifying speed until suddenly it stopped, motionless and sacred, above a pointed rock in front of
Francis. It was a fiery figure with wings, nailed to a cross
of fire. Two flaming wings rose straight upward, two others opened out horizontally, and two more covered the
figure. And the wounds in the hands and feet and heart
were blazing rays of blood. The sparkling features of the
Being wore an expression of supernatural beauty and

grief. It was the face of Jesus, and Jesus spoke. Then suddenly streams of fire and blood shot from His wounds and pierced the hands and feet of Francis with nails and his heart with the stab of a lance. As Francis uttered a mighty shout of joy and pain, the fiery image impressed itself into his body, as into a mirrored reflection of itself, with all its love, its beauty, and its grief. And it vanished within him. Another cry pierced the air. Then, with nails and wounds through his body, and with his soul and spirit aflame, Francis sank down, unconscious, in his blood.

—From A Treasury of Catholic Reading, ed. John Chapin (Farrar, Straus & Cudahy, 1957)

Not only is blood seen and utilized as a path that leads to enlightenment, but pain as well. One sect of the Dervishes in Arabia known as the Rufai, or 'Howling Dervishes' also use blood and pain to elevate their minds to a state of heightened spiritual awareness called 'Melboos'. Another well known Sufi sect is the 'Swirling Dervishes' who spin round until a trance is laid upon them and they find union with 'God' which they view as life itself and interestingly, that they themselves are 'God' as well. Unlike the Swirling Dervishes, the Rufai are known to inflict physical pain upon themselves in place of 'swirling', to enter into melboos so that they may commune with 'God', or the self in a heightened spiritual trance state.

...The Rufai, or Howling Dervishes who slash their bodies with knives and burn themselves with red-hot irons... In Not only is blood seen and utilized as a path that leads to enlightenment, but pain as well. One sect of the Dervishes in Arabia known as the Rufai, or 'Howling Dervishes' also use blood and pain to elevate their minds to a state of heightened spiritual awareness called 'Melboos'. Another well known Sufi sect is the 'Swirling

Dervishes' who spin round until a trance is laid upon them and they find union with 'God' which they view as life itself and interestingly, that they themselves are 'God' as well. Unlike the Swirling Dervishes, the Rufai are known to inflict physical pain upon themselves in place of 'swirling', to enter into melboos so that they may commune with 'God', or the self in a heightened spiritual trance state.

...The Rufai, or Howling Dervishes who slash their bodies with knives and burn themselves with red-hot irons... In front of them was a brazier, with a glowing bed of charcoal, from which emerged the handles of knives, long iron pins, like spits, with wooden handles, and iron pokers with no handles at all.

—W.B. Seabrook, 'Adventures In Arabia', 1927

This scene is also described by Seabrook:

"Suddenly one of the Dervishes leaped to his feet, threw off his cloak, leaped again into the air, naked to the waist. The Rufai sheik leaped up at the same time, seized a long, red-hot spit by its wooden handle from the brazier, and began waving it wildly in the air...the other Dervish circled, leaping around the sheik and howling, then backed, with his head pressed sideways against the wooden pillar, with his mouth gaping open, and stood rigid, motionless. The sheik inserted the spit at an angle into his mouth, and with a solid blow of his fist drove it through the man's cheek and pinned him to the pillar."~ W.B. Seabrook, 'Adventures In Arabia', 1927

I have personally experienced a very similar ritual where I rose above the pain that was inflicted, and became 'one' with the Universe. I was fortunate to be in a circle of friends who were suspension artists, and one night I was given the rare opportunity to partake in one of their sacred rites. I was pierced with two six gauge, four-foot-long crisscrossing spears through my back and one six gauge, two foot long spear through both cheeks with my mouth open, (very much like the Dervish as described) as well as two more smaller 10 gauge needles pierced through my lower lip. I now intimately relate to this particular kind of unique experience in the quest for finding oneself, or 'God'.

When in such a state, reality is suspended and in place of feeling pain, one rises above it and 'rides' it. The intense pain thrusts the mind and spirit into a state of excitement where ones extra sensory mode is activated and one not only feels life around him, but 'sees' life around him. The energy that resonates off a person while experiencing this transcendent state is quite amazing, it's as if they are 'cracked' open and the energy that lies beneath their material 'shell' radiates out as a star burning its brightest and hottest before it goes out, as the rituals usually don't last more than an hour. It is something I find difficult to describe, as it is such a personal experience, and differs from one individual to another. Though, one thing that is always universally experienced among practitioners is the spiritual feeling of freedom, being alive and connected to all, in a moment frozen in time.

These are just a few examples of the use of blood and pain within different cultures and religious movements of the world. There are many, many more examples, as blood is seen as symbolic for a great multitude of religions and spiritual reasons ranging from life and death, to being purified to unclean. Of course, Pagans and Magicians also view blood as a spiritual essence, though it is seen as something more personal that does not belong to a God, but to them. It is embraced as life, but also serves as a reminder of death, being seen as magical, having unique properties that can be utilized in many different ways concerning ritual and as an agent in contacting spiritual entities. This is age old tradition still being put to use by many modern practitioners and occult orders, especially in the rapidly growing LHP movement along with the new interest in the Afro-Brazilian religious traditions, such as Quimbanda, Palo Mayombe and Voudon.

Personally, I use blood in many rituals and workings, I always have. It is something very sacred to me. In my eyes, it serves as a sign of devotion as well as sacrifice. Within my spiritual beliefs, I kneel before no God, though offer them my essence out of respect and to empower the rite. I see most entities as being equal, some have been here longer than me and have more knowledge and experience, but that does not make them superior to me, only more learned. And, as more learned, they should know this and have the same respect for me, as I do them, equally. Else, why would I commune with them as spiritual brothers? I offer them sacrifice, not out of fear, but honor and respect. I beg no entity or God to change things in my life, I ask them to help me as a brother, who walks the same crooked path as they do, and if I can help them in turn, then I gladly do.

My first use of blood in magic was when I was in my teenage years; (buying what I could of magic books that were to be found at the bookstore in the mall) no system that I had found then really resonated with me, so I created my own from elements I did resonate with, from within various systems. I didn't realize at the time that I had just taken my first step on the path to becoming a Chaos Magician. I came to understand that the one dominate reoccurring magical factor in my life was the moon, I was drawn unnaturally (or supernaturally) to the moon. Not only that, but huge life changing events would occur on the first three nights of the waxing crescent moon, to the point that the connection could not be ignored, even by the most skeptical. Therefore, I began honoring it as a sentient being, and quickly found that my life was infused with incredible luck and magic, as if all life's doors were suddenly open, and I could walk through whichever ones I chose at my leisure with ease.

I would take a wooden box that served as my alter, that I had painted with various symbols (some known, and others my own) along with my ritual supplies, up to the top of a large wooded hill that overlooked the city. It was quite beautiful and I would often encounter deer and other wildlife on my journey upward. Once there I would lie out my alter and tools, light the alter candle and meditate on my current position in life, what was important and that which I desired to change. I then would cut my left arm with a clean razorblade three times, deep enough to let blood flow just a trickle (there is always such a spiritual release that I experience when this occurs, it is no different for me now then it was for me then) and spread a good amount of blood on a dead leaf that I had procured on the trip up the mountain. Once done, I would burn the leaf so that my essence would entwine with the energy of the night as the smoke would rise to caress the moon. At that point in the ritual I would partake of the blood myself, enjoying tasting the raw energy of life itself dance upon my tongue...As said, I had tremendous positive results with this, and still do when practiced, though the ritual has grown to encompass much more meaning and depth.

Of course, now that I am older and have experienced more than what the new age books of the mall had to offer, I work with blood in a more complex way. I have found that spiritual activity is greatly increased when blood is used in ritual. I find this because the energy that is being released by the magician acts as a beacon in the spiritual world, attracting many different curious entities. It is such a personal offering that the magician can fully immerse himself in ritual and the spiritual world, so contact with an entity is stronger and a bond formed.

Naturally, blood is also used in a lot of sigil work I undertake. I believe blood helps to bring 'Life' to a sigil if created with it. This of course again connects the magician with the spiritual entity that is being called forth, creating a pact of sorts as it is the essence of the magician (blood), conjoined with the essence of the spirit (sigil). I see ritual as something very private that takes place between myself and the spirits, something that others should not see. It is a time when my earthly skin is shed, and my spiritual being can fully breathe in the night and embrace the spirits on their ground. It is something sacred and beautiful, and should be respected and seen as such. When one works with blood, spirits, and the night, an amazing collage of magic is painted upon the canvas of reality, immersing the magician in a state of non-reality where the miraculous is able to be brought forth into the magician's plane of awareness.

This twilight of the in-between is where magic is performed, it is where time and space cease to exist and action occurs.

In my book, 'Volubilis Ex Chaosium', blood is used to draw the Old Ones close:

> Throughout the history of magic, blood has been used as a means to attract spirits and to be used as an energy source for them to materialize into visible appearance before the magician. Blood is used in these workings as an energy source for the Old Ones to be drawn to the Trinity of Triangles so that interaction may occur, in whatever form it may take. Blood is the eternal energy and essence of all life. It is the most sacred and personal offering that one can make to the Gods. There are many examples of the use of blood sacrifice in 'Yog~Sothothery', and is definitely a reoccurring theme when evocation of a said entity is to be called forth. Therefore staying true to Lovecraft's visions, it has been employed in this magical system.

I have found the spiritual interaction within V.E.C., very powerful and effective, as it deals with the very 'edge' or outer realms of the magical Universe in experimental realms such as the 'Tunnels of Set' also known as the 'Vaults of Zin', or what may be called the 'Nagual' (drawing from Don Juan's terminology), though it still utilizes traditional ritual elements within its structure. And, within this system, blood and pain are used, as in the 'Nyarlathotep Initiation Ceremony', as a way to both heighten and excite the spiritual mind of the magician to a level of awareness that is needed for communion with the Old Ones.

There are also a great many who hold the belief that ingesting blood infuses one with spiritual strength or 'energy', resulting in vampiric qualities including heightened senses both spiritually and physically, as well as immortality of either the physical or ethereal body. There have been many throughout history who have been known to utilize blood as an element for the rejuvenation of life. One of the most famous; Elizabeth Bathory, was known to have bathed in, and drank, the blood of over 650 young women in efforts to remain young and live forever. There are reports stating that her desired end result of youth was somewhat achieved, until she was jailed of course.

Though, through the ages a division has been made manifest between the material and the spiritual aspects of blood. There are now recognized vampires who only consume the 'Life Force', or 'Prana' of a person that is carried by the blood throughout the body, rather than ingesting the blood itself, this is well known as psychic vampirism. 'The Temple Of The Vampire' is one such religion which recognizes this praxis as a core pillar in their religious construct.

They hold the belief that they are evolved humans who drink in the personal energy of lesser humans and store it. When enough energy is collected, they enter into a ritual they call 'Communion' where they freely release all their stored energy to the 'Undead Gods' in return for the Undead Gods to release their Vampiric energy upon them. With each transfusion of life-force, they become less human, taking on the qualities of their ascended masters.

The Vampiric Condition is, therefore, a condition of
evolution actualized by the exchange of Life-force energy with
Those Who Have Risen (The Undead Gods) above the
restriction of a physical body.

—T.O.T.V., 'Revelations', 2006

However within their Temple, blood drinking is looked
down upon:

Drinking physical blood is a socially unacceptable behavior and reveals a deep misunderstanding of our religion.

—T.O.T.V.,'Website', 2012

Although this view is not always agreed upon between Vampires and the personal beliefs they hold, and therefore the practice of blood drinking as an energy source is still utilized by many
underground societies as well as in individual solitary praxis:

"The grand fantasy that many would be vampires have in
these modern times is that the physical consumption of blood is
wholly unnecessary for the vampire's maintenance of immortal
existence. This is a basic fallacy stemming from the most recent
resurgence in the occult movement of the 1990's...'The simple truth of the matter is that the vampire must, in conjunction
with vital energy manipulation, (which begins with techniques
of visualization) consume large quantities of food that contains
exceedingly high amounts of life-force, prana, etc'...'Now, the
truth of the matter is that human blood, being the substance of
life for the most highly cognitive and evolved species on this
planet, contains the most concentrated degree of life-force available." ~ A.W. Dray, 'Nox Infernus', 2011

The spectrum for the uses of blood in the areas of religion
and magic is vast. Another area of interest is the use of blood as
a medium for divination. The specific name or names for this are
'Hematomancy' or 'Haematomancy', which breaks down to,

Haimat = Blood, and Manteia = Prophecy. Dririmancy is specifically divination by observing dripping blood and the patterns it creates upon whatever surface is being utilized in the ritual. One similar method of spiritual contact that can be utilized, is the use of blood in conjunction with mirrors to open gateways. This is seen in an anonymous rite that was included in Scarlet Imprint's, "Diabolical". The practitioner adorns a full length mirror with demonic sigils drawn of their own blood, especially where the infernalist's face and heart will appear in the reflection. Once done, the Demon is evoked/invoked into the reflection of the magician. This is a very effective operation, as it again relates to connecting the magician to the spirit being called forth through the mirror, by the use of sigils and blood. As stated, this type of bond formed with a spiritual entity is amazingly strong and cannot be easily broken.

Blood...We instinctively know its strength, we feel its seductive rhythm pounding through the world as the drums of destiny pushing us ever forward into the 'Night of Times', pounding as our hearts beat within our own chests, breathing life within our flesh and making 'Alive', that which would not be. For it is the blood of 'God'...of 'Self'...of 'Being' that courses through our veins and bestows upon us the very fragile and easily extinguished flame we call existence. Drink in its essence, feel it flow through you, for this is magic in its purest and strongest form, a magic that ever changes as the raging force of untamed Chaos itself. ✶

Becoming Hoodoo

PART TWO

Kyle Fite

The action of the Paraclete...will extend to the principle of generation. The divine life will sanctify the organs which henceforth procreate only elect creatures, exempt from original sin, creatures whom it will not be necessary to test in the fires of humiliation, as the Holy Bible says. This was the doctrine of Vintras...the doctrine has been continued and amplified, since Vintras's death, by his successor, Dr. Johannes."

— The Astrologer Gevingey in discourse with Durtal and Des Hermies from J.K. Huysmans' *La Bas*

1

THOSE familiar with the biographical details surrounding the writing of Huysmans' La Bas will know that its author was personally acquainted with the Abbe Joseph-Antoine Boullan, who was represented within that tale as the character Dr. Johannes. This is an important fact for us to bear in mind as Boullan's detractors painted him as a grotesque blasphemer immersed in the most perverse practices of a sexual

and satanic nature. These detractors included several propo-
nents of "white magic," such as Oswald Wirth who, along with
Stanislas de Guaita, disingenuously sought tutelage from Boullan in order to infiltrate his Sanctum Sanctorum at the highest
level and thereby discover the truth of his allegedly wicked work.

That Boullan was concerned with those energies infusing
"the principle of generation" is not in question. The nature of
his practice, however, has not only been maligned by his enemies, it has been embraced in its tabloid misrepresentations by
misguided persons seeking to emulate the shadow of a "Satan-
ist" who never existed. We find Huysmans to be a much more
accurate representative of the eminent "Dr. Johannes" than
those who, reacting to his insight into the sexual nature of divine
magic, condemned him as being in league with the devil, setting
off a chain reaction of lurid gossip and speculation which has all
but shrouded the mission of this almost forgotten priest.

Boullan was a proponent of a philosophy-and rite-which he
called "The Union of Life." This outlook saw all Being partici-
pating in the Growth and Action of One Being. The One Being
referred to is God and therefore All Life is regarded as part of
the Body of God. In addressing the problems of mortal manifestation, we are challenged to understand and act in accord with
the proper relationship between these parts whereby the whole
is most freely expressed in Time. This forms a link between
Time and Eternity which finds expression in the figure of Jesus
Christ, the "God- Man."

The conceit of man (actively encouraged to this day by aber-
rant theologies) is put into check by this philosophy. As "Boulla-
nists," we do not see ourselves as sanctioned by some divine de-
cree to trample over all creation as Christic consumers. With the
Holy Scriptures declaring that all things were put on earth for
man's use, we have seen the rise of a twisted religious justification for abuse of all creation. With the proclamation that the

righteous will one day judge the angels, we observe the establishment of a demented superiority complex. Human beings have made of themselves little suns around whom the universe revolves. While thinking we glow with glory, we have actually become enchained in a state of stunted growth, behaving as infants when the same scriptures we quote (to adorn our ignorance) also tell us to put away childish things, moving from the "milk" to "meat" of wisdom.

The Union of Life is a sexual philosophy wherein we relate to all forms of life within the Continuum of Reality. We become a vehicle of the Lord of the Crossroads as we form a living link in the connective chain between the "lower" and the "higher." This is a volitional position. Our contact with the "inferior" is meant to raise that life-condition to the level of our own just as our contact with the "superior" is meant to raise our own life-condition. Contact alone does not facilitate this process. As alluded to above, we can abuse those powers we think of as beneath us. We may, likewise, form imbalanced and destructive relationships with those powers we conceive of as "transcendental." Major world religions have grown and been sustained within this psychosis. In Boullan's teachings, effective relationships between Life-Levels are based in an awareness of necessary interconnectedness as well as the matrix in which that interconnectedness functions.

Within the Lucky Hoodoo Cult aligned with the Boullan Academy of Spiritual Service (itself a body aligned with the occult activities of OTOA-LCN), the Union of Life forms the central teaching whereby Hoodoo Science is directed towards Inner Plane Communion with the Ancestral and Atlantean Spirits. We are Masonic in understanding how the True Temple of Sol-Om-On is fashioned from Living Stones. Through the Gnosis of this Metaphor, we go beyond simply thinking that we are lifting up the Lower while being exalted within the Higher. We literally become the vehicle whereby the Higher communicates with the Lower. This is Christian in the Esoteric sense of the word where a Christian is understood to be "Little Christ" in the World. One must live out the Christ-Drama in his or her life as a Hoodoo. This is not some linear sequence of events traced through Biblical narrative but a superstructure into which we project our karmas for an adjustment that also adjusts the World.

2

It is a difficult thing to express a Cosmic Sexuality to one who understands Sexuality solely in terms of the animal body. It is even more difficult when one regards the animal condition as a blight on the spiritual path. Thus it was that Boullan's teachings concerning the Union of Life were slandered by "critics" who suggested that he was providing justification for all manner of evil, including bestiality. Such is the outlook left for those who can only understand sex in terms of the mammalian man's corporeal body. Our view is not one that eschews this-but it must be noted that human bio-sexuality is only one of myriad expressions of Cosmic Sexuality. Even within our flesh, Sexuality takes on an infinitude of forms. In fact, we will not be amiss to honor this primordial force in EVERY aspect of human existence. The mingling of one thought with another and the new thought arising from this union...this is also sexuality!

Within our Hoodoo Shadowverse, our thought-life does not simply interact with itself. It extends outward and connects into a vast sea of intelligence around us. The Atlantean Awareness residing within each and all of us seeks empowerment through the acramental technology of the Union of Life whereby its continuous copulation with all phenomena may be both sanctified and fruitful. This gives insight into why the sex magic operations known within the Crowleyan system as the 8th, 9th and 11th Degrees are preceded by the 7th in which sexual energy is related to ere it is directed into expression.

The Key is to enter into a full body-mind awareness of the sex- force beyond its particular expression via the human bio-organism. When this is achieved, one's bodily actions may be imbued with the Gnostic influx which is universally radiant. Many curious and intrepid magicians desire to "learn the secrets" of these so-called "upper grades." Hoodoo Science holds the Key whereby these "Operations" reveal themselves. One does not need an Order to explain this magic nor does one who has entered these Mysteries require a human affirmation of attainment. The Monastery of the Seven Rays serves its students on the Path towards the 7th Degree which, after a manner, is the Highest Degree one may enter in human form. If one has formed a conception of the Qabalistic Grades based on linear consciousness, this statement will sound like admittance to partial knowledge. Let me say this: the Abyss will destroy linear consciousness along with all other modes of consciousness. Entry therein may prove to be a Gateway to insanity-or Supersanity. Despite its dangers, we don't feel that this "Crossing" need be some dread event. It is the natural and inevitable trajectory of the Soul. The Abyss may also be regarded as the Atlantean Deep. This is more than mere metaphor. We are diving the depths of our most extreme karmic past that we may realize our most vital future through magical acceleration in the present.

3

HOODOO LOG

Longing for more than the occlusion of modern materialistic consciousness, I strike a match, light a colored candle and begin my voyage.

Many who begin work with the coursework of Michael Bertiaux's Lucky Hoodoo Grimoire have expressed to me frustration when they don't immediately experience the "bells and whistles" they were hoping for. This is not an issue of failure but a simple need for adjustment in consciousness.

I do not shove expectation onto the Hoodoo any more than I would my earthly friends. I have called up my faith and feel tremendous gratitude for the ability to do so. I simply know that the Spirits are present and my Love eclipses any need for performance on their part. We join in the Field of Love. I open to the Presence of Hoodoo and my Soul is thereby opened to the Presence of God. God is not obligated to manifest in some expected or longed for guise. God has never been unmanifest and therefore I simply open my Being to God. That flame flickering on the candle's wick is God manifest. Do I require more? I am seeing the Salamander in physical manifestation and it silently chants praise to the Lord.

The wax-feeding flame dance is no more a manifestation of God than the thought-life I identify as being "in my head." There is some vague and hazy notion of a scaly form sweeping by me in an oily black space. My rational mind springs forward to target and dispel the form. It is "just imagination," it declares. But it is wrong. This imaginative form is a type of body-a vehicle-through which the Hoodoo are moving. The Rational Mind may as well tell me that my body is "just a body" and, being subject to perpetual change and dissolution without any substantial existence, should be disregarded, along with all its reports. But its reports are all that sustains the Rational Mind and knowing this, the RM retreats to a corner to gnaw its knuckles. Soon it will meet the Gravewalker Without Hands.

Meanwhile, I am taken down into darkness so thick, I cannot determine if there is water or air about me. I cannot tell if I yet live or have died. The darkness gives way to flashings (electrical storm between these two elements) and I enter a world of terrors with a strange detachment. Were I wholly in my bodily soul, I would surely recoil. Instead I drift forward, through carnage and carnality. What I behold doesn't require description. Suffice to say that it is sufficient to punch holes through fears I never knew I had. This is no horror movie. It is a custom-tailored vision quest in which all my walls come tumbling down. What is ugly for me may be a cake-walk for you, dear reader. And vice versa, certainly. It's enough to say that I'm stabbed where I bleed. There will be no tribal scars to tribute my manhood. The blood-flow is like a thread being pulled to unravel my entire Self-concept. The Tibetans call this the Bardo. Padmasambhava's revelations were beamed in from Bon Po Time Travelers. And the Bon Po? They were Tibet's Hoodoo Technicians.

4

Let's talk Skulls. One of my earliest childhood memories was being at a grocery store and looking at the small toy selection by the magazine rack. One of these toys was Ghost Rider. It may have been the first time I saw Ghost Rider. I knew nothing of the comic book saga and was simply seeing a little plastic man on a motorcycle with a flaming skull for a head. I was duly impressed. This was one of the coolest things I had seen in my young life.

The Skull is chic. I have one tattooed on my arm. Those empty eyes, that toothy grin. Somehow sinister and humorous at the same time, the Skull is both badass and gothic groovy. Traditional forms of the Great Baron arise and I find myself thinking "Allright, now we're talking!"

The Tibetans are the Biker Gang of the Spirit-World. Their leather jackets are Thangkas. Malas are a chain in the fist. It was, in fact, Mahakala who called me to Buddhism, announcing the existence of religion in which the flaming skull was a Mystery. I dove into the Book of the Dead and thence to Zazen. But it was a vat of hydrochloric-and not lysergic-acid that I would find myself sitting in. I was a fish lunging for the worm on a hook. I was also the fisherman. And I was caught.

When I enter the Graveyard below the worlds, the Baron knows better than to hand me some Halloween mask. What he reveals freezes the blood in my veins. This is not some Hollywood thrill- trip. I meet my loved ones and watch as the ignominy of death drapes itself over those I cherish most. The lovely scent of skin turns sour and the soul flees, leaving me with dull and unresponsive clay. Eyes that once met mine in a darting flash now stare, fish-like, idiot and blind. I am not afraid of the quickly rotting flesh. Grieving overrides horror. I am more than alive even as my heart is collapsing in my chest. The Baron has touched me and my blood has turned black.

I look into his face, draped in the worm-eaten flesh of innocence. I become a dog, snarling spittle at the puppet-people who jerk about on strings and think themselves daringly dancing at some sexy party for esoteric extremists. I am eating my own heart pressed into the form of a broken body, a vessel which once emanated Light. I try to find a glimmer in its inmost warmth and instead crack ice-cubes against my teeth.

I crash through some Tran-spatial membrane and see a Haitian woman wailing with her half-a-boy cradled in trembling arms. Earthquake. It tends to break a body. And broken bodies tend to break a heart.

America bays for the entertainment of torture porn and yet a single tear from this nameless mother's eye rips through the silver screen, announcing a wound that will never heal. I cannot smell the stink of putrefaction as such loss is measured against love.

Histories evaporate beneath cruel suns. Love pulls nails up through hands not yet cruciform. I am father to Herod's victim. My best friends die the stupidest of deaths. The hateful foe takes his place alongside blood clots, wrong turns and chicken bones. I vomit up unspoken words and am bound in chains of remorse.

Each tooth in the Baron's head tells a thousand tales at once. He reveals his great power to heal and preserve as he continuously patches me up to withstand the next round of bullets to the gut.

He retreats now-and yet his face remains. I am holding a mirror. Somewhere, someone is cutting a deal for sex, for money. Someone is praising the ancient ones for a fresh box of vanity delivered Fed-Ex. Might as well credit Jesus for the business merger, the vote, the touchdown.

Me? I am Becoming HOODOO.

As the Atlantean Adepts returned from the Great Deluge, so the Dead shall rise again in the Resurrection wherein Universe Z(ombi) is known in our Gnosis as Universe Z(othyria).

5

We tend to think of our bodies as the dense, tangible and gross portion of what we are. Our "souls" are conceived of as something more light, ethereal and refined. I would encourage the interested reader to take an afternoon and enjoy C.S. Lewis' story The Great Divorce. In this powerful fantasy, Lewis, as narrator and protagonist, arrives in Heaven to find himself, still imperfect and underdeveloped, to be as a ghost compared to the astounding SOLIDNESS of the spiritual world around him. It takes time to adjust to the vibratory level of Heaven and grow into its reality. By the same token, our Hoodoo Life is not some shadowy corner of the mind called up as an accoutrement to our baseline self. It IS the baseline self.

There are many techniques to come into this awareness. The important thing is to get there. Entry into this zone is a True Initiation which will enable us to engage with our magical work as a critical component of our innermost being. One literally "wakes up" and crawls out of the coffin. Timezones connect within the flesh and there is no question concerning destiny. Awareness and Action supplant speculation. You are no longer a human being seeking contact with entities who may or may not be "real." You ARE an entity.

Wearing a skull in place of a face, your space-spanning sight is no longer occluded by the vegetative vision of twin flesh orbs. Emerging into the Gnosis of the Union of Life, you find creatures and intelligences petitioning YOU in the same way you sought spirit-contact with candles and incense. As you respond, you see how those otherworldly ones who once bent your reality tunnel are, likewise, turning towards their "Elders" for direction on the Path. This vision then buckles and dimensionalizes .

No being can be a dot on a line. The continually morphing matrices of Being evoke a multitude of relations. That "inferior" we are lifting up is now seen as our Most Holy Guru, well-disguised and raising us through the actions of service and compassion. This same Guru is being lifted into Awareness beyond our comprehension by virtue of this interaction with US. Outside of time, we are Guru to the Guru and the Universe is Chela to Itself.

6

HOODOO LOG

Watched the E. J. Gold video on Youtube discussing the "Body Of Habits" last night and was struck by the words in the echo-chamber at the end. That first and important question: "Am I alive...or am I dead?" This morning I'm driving to work and, like a ball bounced down into my mind-strata, those words come back. "Am I alive...or am I dead?" Well, how am going to determine this? I check my breathing. Yep, still going. But here's the thing: when the thought occurred to me to observe my breathing, I WASN'T BREATHING. It was almost as if my lungs were suddenly springing to life and sucking down a chestload of air IN RESPONSE to my unspoken inquiry. I repeated the same experiment later on in the day. Same thing.

What does this tell me?

It tells me that there is no breathing going on when I am not paying attention to it. I can tell myself it must be so-and then accept my own persuasive words. Of course, I must be right, right? Why, all the people around me would vouchsafe my reason and we all know that popular opinion is to be relied on in all matters of life and death. After all, the majority mind has such wonderful and certain convictions re: God, the Universe and what is Right and Wrong. And look at the way they've sur-mounted all world problems with this wisdom. If it weren't for them, we'd still be struggling with class division, poverty, crime and all the petty shit that once spread itself all over a Day In The Life Of A Human.

But there remains something inside of me which is perenni-ally perturbed. Call me a malcontent. But the same crew has as-sured me since I was a boy that I hasten towards a fate where worms will burrow into my brain and my lifeless arms stand no chance of doing a coffin crawl back to the wake world. Despite the overwhelming success in manifesting Heaven On Earth-and answering all ontological inquiries with satisfying reply-I smell a rat. I clawed at the walls and ripped through all the drywall in the house to get its maddening screeching to stop. Alas, the rat had made its home elsewhere. I finally cut it out of my head us-ing some basic kitchen utensils. If anything, I ask you to be im-pressed with this. It was NOT easy and I lost an eye in the pro-cess.

Of course, it would turn out that the eye was my end of a bargain. A raven carried it off as I flailed around on my front lawn clutching my face like some loser in a slasher flick.

So, where was I? Oh yeah. I had a towel stuffed into my or-bital socket and was blowing blood bubbles from my nose. And the rat was dead.

And then I was in my car, heading to work and thinking of Mr. Gold's video. My lungs were more than happy to oblige my attention. In truth, everything was. The grass turned green as I looked at it. Cars painted themselves different colors as they passed me by. My office assembled itself into a mass of moving people and it all looked so...natural.

Just like that well-painted corpse in the coffin. God, we never saw her look better.

And like me, she wasn't even breathing.

So, it only takes a few minutes on the internet and my morning routine to turn me into a solipsist. But being the unsatisfied bastard that I am, I now eye that philosophy with suspicion. It's another rat in the house. At least it won't be looking to make a nasty nest in my head. Even rodents have to be wary of what's left above my shoulders.

AM I ALIVE OR AM I DEAD?

Would I even KNOW? And if so, how? You see this is the piss- poor logic of the pedestrian: If I'm aware of myself having some sort of existence, then I must be alive. Who reasons like this? Apparently, the human race. The same gang who must, assuredly, have had occasion to reason, by contrast, that they have been dead, also. Such convincing arguments for this.

Then again, I have played around a little with magic. A ritual here or there. I even did one where I opened my being to the "Hoodoo

Spirits" and entered a binding contract with them for all eternity. Call me impetuous. If the Devil ever wants to buy my soul, I'll be skipping off like the guy who scored a ten spot for the Brooklyn Bridge.

Who are the Hoodoo? Well, if we start with Baca Bacalou's Grimoire-transmitted through that eminent Chicago medium, the Reverend Michael Bertiaux, we'll know they are the Super-Team composed of the transmigrated Atlantean Magi and our Necro- friends from the Zombi Realm. No, it's really not any stranger than the idea that we are animated flesh-husks composed of "Atoms" who hop about on a whirling marble which repeatedly encircles an incomprehensibly large gas-ball. We've all got our own Mythos. The question is: where is it getting us?

Eventually, for the Big Lucky Hoodoo, this gang takes up residence in the body. Lucky for them, I've evicted the vermin.

I don't mind being the Landlord. I provide space and they AL-WAYS pay rent on time. We also have great conversations down at the office.

7

Kyle: So, Dead Dudes, is it really possible that...I'm one of you?

DD: Humans are infants in the Great Cosmic Nursery. Look at how they turn the Soul inside out and embrace their inverted vision with ferocity. We've witnessed their racist idealism with alternating disgust and amusement. Not one of them could pick out their chosen "pure-blood" in a room where we've plucked the feathers from the chickens.

K: Plucked the feathers from the chickens?

DD: Flayed them all.

K: So, um, how does this answer my question?

DD: We flay more than flesh. In fact, we show those with eyes to see how there is no flesh to be flayed. How do you think we escaped the Great Deluge?

K: OK, I think I get your point. Life is a type of Illusion and we need to see through this to enter into the Gnosis of the Death.

DD: Kyle, this is just one half of the equation. Could not Death also be the illusion that we "need to see through" to enter into the Gnosis of Life?

K: Well, sure. That sounds very...mystical.

DD: Fuck your ideas about mysticism. The few humans who truly approach us behold our HOO-DOO Forms only because of their personal polarity. Remember, you contact us with candles to the West and North. But when we have brought you into our World, you are lighting candles at all four quarters.

K: So, am I dead?

DD: There is no death, Kyle Fite. Even when your loved ones behold your body dropping its temp and turning back to clay, there is no death. Even as you are fed into a furnace, there is no death. So what remains? Life? Yes, it is LIFE. BUT-! Most humans have no understanding of what LIFE IS. They operate in context of an ILLU-SION OF LIFE which is why they behave like petulant brats at the expense of each other's existence.

K: Then what IS "Life?" DD: Life is Reality.

K: What is Reality?

DD: Reality is what you imagine.

K: Reality is what I imagine it to be???

DD: No, Dumb-Ass. That's not what we said. Reality is what you IMAGINE.

K: How is this so?

DD: You can know nothing beyond Imagination. The English poet, William Blake, knew this and proclaimed it as Gospel. He knew us, also. He simply called us "Fa-erie." We empowered William Blake and invited him to witness one of our funerals.

K: But-what about all the Buddhist shtick? You know, going beyond the forms we imagine to get to the Pure Light of Reality? You, yourself, said that all this Life and Death business is an illusion.

DD: Yes, we know the Buddha very well. He is one of our Adepts.

K: The historic Guatama is a Hoodoo?

DD: No, Kyle. He's a BIG LUCKY HOODOO!

K: So how is Reality Imagination?

DD: You owe us some rum.

K: (scrambles for the booze)

DD: (slurps it down) You DO realize rum is metaphor?

K: But you just drank it all!

DD: (obnoxious belch)

K: ...

DD: There can be no experience outside of Imagination. All you know of "fact" is imagined. This is your "grass turning green as you observe it." This is your lungs springing to life as you ask if you're alive. "Knowing" belongs to the World of Imagination. Without image, there is no knowledge. Image can never embrace a totality and therefore it must always be subjective. Despite this, the subjectivity of image is generated from an encounter within the objective continuum of Reality. We can answer your philosophic inquiry because it belongs to the realm of subjectivity. You can ask nothing from objectivity. Objectivity does not ask questions. Questions belong to the realm of the subjective mind as a vehicle of experience.

K: So what is the relation between the Subjective and Objective?

DD: We have said that Subjectivity is the vehicle of experience. But what is doing the "experiencing?"

K: The Objective.

DD: Well, there's hope for you after all.

End of Part Two ✶

Gargophias

The Fundamentals of Utilizing the Qliphoth to Perfect Being of Becoming in Nothingness/Everything in the Path Transfixed of the Void
Angela Edwards

AS a practitioner of the Left Hand Path and as an artist. I have always been fascinated by the role of psychosexual transgression. Through extremes and the role of in these things sacred prostitution/female psychosexuality.

This type of work I have physically undertaken. It has been directly related the ideology of through ritual. Using the tunnels and Sephiroth of the Qliphoth (Tree of Death). In these practices the left hand path is not evil as such. When relating to right hand path ideology or philosophy. Both are neither good or bad in the profane misconception and both work towards the same goal of being united with the spirits. Or to a higher universal understanding.

The LHP's only difference is to my mind that it involves full surrender in embracing all shedding the skin, pushing one's own boundaries in the world. For it is the active path of FIRE of full becoming also.

In the actions of experiencing through choice, extreme sexuality or violence in my rituals. Sperm, female discharge and blood are all used to activate these radical uncompromising highways. Using the Left Hand Path rituals of abolishing all through sex creation and death blood sacrificed wholly.

That in the practitioner's descent of full surrender of oneself to the depths. Transform him/her to the practitioner's full ascension of untainted divinity.

To reach our fully activated by the radiating black sun than empowers the abyss. Our Luciferian full nature revealed.

The void of spirituality or consciousness. As I would see it the world's computer to the root of all. The void is another aspect found in the daemon Choronzon a elemental explored in Setian philosophy. In the work of Thomas Karlsson (Qabalah, Qliphoth and Goetic magic). Also Choronzon can be linked directly to the void. As Choronzon is said to be a gateway to the Qliphothic universe. That this daemon acts as a control panel of energy translating as the void. The universal light that operates the Abyss. This philosophy regarding these elements and aspects of Choronzon's character. Are reiterated in the Typhonian grimoire The Nightside of Eden By Kenneth Grant. Grant describes Choronzon as the gateway to the Qliphoth. The governing energy that operates all transmissions and access for the practitioner into the void, Abyss and Qliphothic realms.

In these aspects Choronzon is characterless and more a reflection of our total darker consciousness. He is also darker universal energy as found in the symbols of Chaos magick. The cause of all transmission and effect. In Chaos magick the teachings are to invoke no Gods or Spirits.

Only universal energy alone to therefore become Choronzon. The ideology of the Chaos magick system. Is the none worship of Gods or higher spirits. We find as practitioners a more purist LHP approach. In placing no superiority on our devotional practice. In all spirits being the voids energy or merged abyss in being nothingness. The Chaos magickal practitioner reaches equality within nothing being sacred to the GODS.

Reflecting the ideology of the LHP adept's philosophy to become merged equal nothingness with the void alone. Using symbolic transmissions that can be traced as the most purist devotional cult of annihilation of human character/ ego in their pure power.

In these aspects Chaos magick is the mother cult of the void and the Abyss. Of supreme magical spiritual attainment of the practitioner crossing over to the spiritual realms fully embraced. Therefore, we could find in the Qliphoth being the dead shells of rebirth to a higher conscious.

The Qliphoth is mainly attributed to belonging to the Chaos magicians work. In magickal contemporary magickal practice today.

For the vat of energy the void can be compared to the black sun or sigil's used in the work of the Chaos magic of Peter Carroll's group the Illuminates Of Thanateros. Or the work of Chaos magic's grandfather Austin O Spare. Who uses his Neither Neither system to become all incorporating divine full gender transcendence. Therefore the womb of the universe that is the void cannot be referred to as neither male or female as at the start and at the end. It is to be to become all incorporated both.

In the grimoire Qutub Chumbley refers to this as the point used in these types of workings. As it being the mother /father to us all of fully embraced transgendered nothingness which in turn is to become our imperfect or perfect uncorrupted nature in the voids prayer invoked.

When the practitioner sheds the skin, surrenders to the flesh, smashes all social conformity.

Pushing the boundaries of gender, sexuality or acceptability in sexual magical ritual they embrace the void also.

This is further explained in abolishment of gender roles within sex magickal practice. And in Crowley's use of the XI degree as a superior form of sexual magick. In Bertiaux's system he refers to this type of sex magical ritual also . Through the red and black alchemical twins or marassas united. In the philosophy of bisexuality/homosexuality being utilised in ritual as the ultimate sex magickal passage. To invocations to higher spiritual attainment.

As Crowley did believe it was only through homosexual passive and dominant anal sex superior magickal powers could be attained. That as he incorporated both sexual roles of giver-taker with his lovers. In becoming male and female sexually united that he would invoke the void or the Abyss. This is explored within his writings extensively including the book The Vision and The Voice. In Crowley's philosophy is similar to the ideas found in Bertiaux's system. In the Voudon Gnostic Workbook.

In VGW Bertiaux also references homosexual passivity merged with homosexual active practices. As his main fundamental sex magickal system. That allows his entrance through the lwa Nibo to access the void.

Through the sephiroth of Uranus which is Daath. This sex magickal practice is by Bertiaux referenced as a means of entering the meon that is the void also. We can also find anal sex or homosexuality explored in similar context. In the work of Kenneth grant. Who refers to this practice in the last of the trilogies (the final attainment of full self through the void) as the mauve zone).

While as a sex magickal practitioner myself I do not see a full relationship with just male homosexual practices or anal sex in particular regarding Qliphoth work etc. Nor do I totally equate these acts. In ritual as doorways in all aspects to the void or abyss transcendence. I have come to the realization that homosexual sex magickal practice. Becomes in theory a example of these practitioners workings to attain through bisexuality or becoming both roles in a sex act male and female. The perfected none gendered aspect of the Qliphoth's work.

In leading to full knowledge of the vision of the void that holds no specific gender. The sexual magickal practitioner is none sexual in that all aspects of sexuality are explored. Regardless of personnel sexual preference to access spirit invocation. In this aspect the prostitute is also none sexual as his or her personnel sexual preferences become irrelevant as regards to their work. This is also a trait found in the switch BDSM who accesses like in bisexuality all aspects of psychosexuality also. In this way all three access the void fully.

As a bisexual woman myself and practitioner. It has been through sexual acknowledgement of all sides of gender male and female taken into myself.

That I have been able to in all sexual magical acts utilize the role of both. Therefore, acknowledge myself as becoming all polarities in this work. Which makes perfect sense when acknowledging that perfect nature attained through the void. That holds no gender in its nothingness.

Therefore, the Qliphoth and void is to become spiritually light activated all things. In this work then type of breakdown occurs of the conditioned self. Where in ritual spiritual contact the practitioner reaches the final stage though consciously embracing these all things to the evolvement of through smashing of ego.

To become transgressed to the void wholly. In reaching the void illuminated by the light of the black sun. Our darker subconscious nature.

We are able to reach in the Luciferian sense of the word our equality with the spirits/GODS outside of humanities restraints.

This end product is the product of full universal gnosis. That is in essence the light bearer lucifer. The one whom, illuminates with shining black sun. In our chosen pathways the true LHP adepts practice. The universes womb is the void of spirit materialization. In these practices of more extreme forms of gnosis and worship lay our true perfect nature.

Our nature as it was before and after, past and future so fully we become. In these types of practice, I have learned that most magic is useless. Without directed real life action and strong projected intent.

For if we are to find our true nature or become the final attainment of as man/woman uniting with the void to higher consciousness. All work should be whether transgression or otherwise. When used as our tools to exploring our true psychosexual nature must be practiced with directed conscious intent. This is the key to all successful magic to practice it with projected true intent.

Another aspect of this practice from my own point of view is that the tunnels of the Qliphoth whether utilized as tools in the ideologies of Grant, Bertiaux, and the Draconian current of the Dragon Rouge. Is that spiritual contact for myself is attained through real life action.

Not just in traditional ritual spirit invocation but in spiritual contact possession within our actions in our material world. In this aspect the spiritual realm crosses over into our mortal realm, so therefore like male/female , sex creation/death , darkness/light all aspects become formed as one .

On the LHPs initiation through surrender sacrifice to all to higher spiritual all embraced attainment. The Qliphoth is the shells of death the void though it is Hebrew the tree of knowledge also.

In this way it is the Abyss of nothingness ruled over by Babalon and all abominations broken also to the divine void. Babalon like some Pomba Giras in the Brazilian religion Quimbanda are identified as being the whore and the ultimate archetype example of the unholy and holy female.

The Qliphoth is activated by the black sun radiating light that the dark light bearer also that is Lucifer uniting Lucifer with Babalon in abyss union wholly.

This is another aspect that fits into the ideologies of Quimbanda as Pomba Gira is the wife of EXU (the Quimbanda lucifer counterpart).

In these spirits we not only find examples of female sexuality, or psychosexuality (as in Lilith often referred as hells whore also) soiled imperfection equating perfection but in the whore that is open to all without judgment. The sacramental spiritual healing unconditional that is also dualistically invoke.

The spirit of Lilith can also be linked to the Quimbanda spirit of Pomba Gira Do Inferno queen of hell fire in Quimbanda. Whom with her chalice (is also linked to the western icon of Babalon). As hells whore again like Lilith who resides upon Malkuth. Minus Liliths colder vampiric manifestations. She is at the roots of the religion of Quimbanda also.

As the original female manifestation of Quimbanda governing all her legions. In being the original imperfect mother of humanities darker aspects as is Lilith.

Lilith hell's whore resides at the base of Malkuth in the Qliphoth's roots that translate as the earth, the holy /unholy filth of universal everything for holy is the WHORE .The whore that in embraced nothingness, nothing remains sacred and all remains sacred in filth .Sacred prostitution is also another aspect of the void.

Not only in that Babalon in Thelema theory sits on the otherside of the Abyss of the void .But in that when working with prostitution that is not sacred in western societies philosophy. That when prostitution becomes used in sacred context it transgresses like the void of nothing to all. Whereupon nothing and everything is sacred wholly.

The connection between the whore who in society is seen as the outcast filth or in sacred whoredom being consciously open to all heals the unwanted, unloved. Who in desperation pay for her services to lay these burdens upon her. The whore becomes the nursemaid to the unwanted masses healing with her filth medicines purity.

When I have been working as a prostitute either on the streets as heroin addicted teenager then later today as a chosen profession to explore its sacred properties consciously as a sex worker and BDSM switch/sub as research towards my second Pomba Gira grimoire writings, film, and paintings. I have found the healing aspect to be true of these actions. In that these actions have informed my magical work. My divine work with Lilith's/Babalon and Pomba Gira currents. As to becoming healing filth and my transgressive Qliphoth work.

With Malkuth's base actions leading to a higher purist gnosis activated by the harsh dark light activated of the black sun. In filth nothing becomes sacred. Therefore, in this path everything within the void becomes sacred also.

In my second experiences of my chosen work of prostitution. Without profane things as circumstance. This has allowed me to wholly give myself over to clients in love or a higher detached understanding from myself sacrifice. In welcoming all human nature no matter how imperfect as beautiful.

This transgressed state of wholly accepting freedom of mind consciousness is the full beauty in ritual translated as the LHP.

In real life actions using sexuality and violence. Examples using cutting of the skin in sigil worship, prostitution, submission all forms of our psychosexual nature. We can in conscious rejection of mundane societies moralistic ideologies surrender ourselves fully to the spirits to all.

To my mind it is not only important to use traditional invocations in spiritual work founded upon classical ritual and our altars. It is of just as much if not more valid importance to transcend traditional spiritual prayer into the living world through our own directed living actions. This includes the practitioner not only in one ritual using cutting as a form of invocation, or anal sex in one sex magical ritual then returning in the profane lives back to normality. Instead it means full surrender to the merciless LHP fully in all areas of their lives day to day.

Living in ritual all transgression ritual practices like for example as found in the Aghori whom sacrifices all worldly possessions to beg upon the street, homelessness or to sleep with corpses in graves out of choice. In a life affirmation extended full ritual.

That in these actions becomes their quest life of full sacrifice also.

For most of the time such approaches to magical work. In western society are rarer. In our culture for most practitioners feel lighting a candle on a altar, reading books or doing a small ritual in a graveyard.

Will be enough to access full spirit contact or spiritual enlightenment. So while all these things are valid in our practice. They are only valid to my mind to a extent. For we need to surrender fully to the LHP. Fully in the action of lifestyle. Living our practices and beliefs. Through real life transgressive rituals or sacrifice ourselves living beyond social conformity. While for some the word lifestyle is a profane terminology. As breaking taboos or transgressing can never become habit or safe. That full transgression should be as in the void in its actions and philosophy the universe limitless .Without manmade restrictions. It is only when fully acknowledged in acceptance in carrying through our beliefs consistently in life. That fully can we become. As outcasts through intent. In our choice to reach full uncompromising Luciferian enlightenment.

To in these acts that incorporate creation sex with death annihilation we can in united alchemical practice reach our soul.

Another aspect of the void or divine nothingness reached through the Qliphoth tree of death knowledge that transgresses to spiritual rebirth. Is that the void can through these rituals when finally rested in or attained translate as the true human soul. The soul to my mind is perfection accomplished through spiritual nothingness, as the soul in my mind human or spiritual transcends the mortal realm in its full ascension totally.

In our infernal path that leads to ascension through regression to the nothingness that is our full realized primal nature in the void.

The full human soul is reached through actions embracing all actions exhibiting the darker sexual, violent aspects of one's nature. In that the soul acknowledges all as worthy or sacred just as in the act of prostitution.

It is open to all rejects nothing as spiritual forms of knowledge or higher spiritual understanding universal enlightenment.

The evolvement of contemporary occultism evolving from more original shamanic forms has I feel regressed upon its self again. For in the voids philosophy and practice as previously discussed access to these Qliphothic universes. Can be only gained by stripping down to the practitioner's body as a vessel only. Therefore, the lowest form of magical vision or practice becomes the highest. The simplistic becomes the most complex.

In that ceremonial magical practice or traditional goetic rituals become worthless. In smashing of all to the divine full nature which lays in the void of full transformation. So we find as practitioners the body that is the shell that covers the soul is to become our only altar. The flesh and blood our tools consecrated in work. As regards through ritual entering the qliphothic void. Of becoming activated universal nothingness which is also ALL.

In the spells of the void all is celebrated. All is sacred in that all is of value to our path to the end magical state which is the Qliphoth state fully activated by the radiating Luciferian black sun in the universe of the void. To reject all gods, take upon yourself no Gods and in this take equality of all gods upon yourself. That is the void invoked. There in the shadows remains light. In this path to perfect being of becoming in the path of nothingness which is also everything the path transfixed of the void alone.

The Conclusion

Black is the Sun: My Eulogy to the Void of Transformation Alone.

Invocation of the Sacred Void

Black is the sun that illuminates the human void. Black is the space that annihilates the ego syringed Black is the sun that radiates enflames my human yearning Black is my sin

Black is my life

Black is my perversion

Black is my blood

Black is my violent, brutality, my honesty.

Black is the sun of full martyred tarnished self-sacrificed sainthood

Black is the depths of the savage unbridled Daemonic Luciferian embodiment.

Black is the sun that illuminates the tunnels of my erotic, violent deprivation

Black rayed is the light that transforms man to divinity

Black is the sun that in its light I find myself crucified through pain to numbness

Black are the sparks that penetrate my eyes, blinded in light were I find my absolution

Black is death in its force of nature

Black is the sun radiating the unidealized human state

Black is the streaming life force of life radiated of dualist acknowledgement of everything.

Black is the sun that illuminates all true life

Black is the light energy streaming through my flesh, bones, body in esoteric activated creative LIVING alchemy

Black is the sun that radiates in uncompromising TRUTH

Black is the humble magician whose only tools of consecration are their bodies, their only altar is the WORLD

Black is the sun that in its energy allows me to be all things embraced without human conscious constraints

Black is the sun that enflames into to thyself empowers

Black is the light that clarifies to glow in all aspects of with FORCE my true soul

Black is the sun high in the universal eros imbued cosmos

Black is the sun that infuses the mages of elemental street nightside magick.

Black is the light upon the dead wastes of the Qliphoth

Black is the sun which trails my left sided bramble spiked pathways

Black is the light that shines upon my life, my pilgrimage.

Black is the light combined that when called upon allows re-birth

Black is the soul shining that I impale upon all my acts, rituals conducted

Black is my transgression state of being

Black is the sun which transforms ugliness to beauty Black
is the sun that hits the dead branches of the tree of death
Black is the sun that abolishes all morals, judgments, em-
braces humble human fragility.

Black is the sun that I bask in to leading to my
full enlightened SOUL.

Black is the sun by which this grimoire is awakened lit Black
is the start that is also the end

Finally, I find black is the Sun of the message in my eulogy
to the void of transformation alone. ✦

Temphioth

Theoretical Demonology in Psychoanalysis
Alexei Dzyuba

What appears as a demon, what is called a demon, what is recognized as a demon, exists within a human being and disappears with him.

— Milarepa, Himalayan yogi (1040-1123).

IT was famous psychologist and mystic Carl Gustav Jung, who began to use mystical metaphors to describe different elements and processes within human psyche. These days, demons are frequently used as metaphors to describe neuroses, even by such pragmatics as NLP-ers.

I would like to analyze the basics if such things as fundamentals of human morality, ethics, and their practically applied functions within human society. Such things, as ethics and morality inevitably come to existence, when the simplest form of society emerges (even though, it may consist only of a few persons). Morality is a code of unwritten (or written) laws and regulations, that directs agreeable, non-conflict functioning of a group of individuals as a whole. This is but glue, or cement, that binds together bricks and guarantees stability of a structure. Certain ethical and moral laws exist among prisoners in a jail, and even in a pack of animals. Scientists, observing social life of chimpanzee, have come to the conclusion, that chimpanzee have very sophisticated political games within their society, that are only slightly less complex, than human politics.

The real purpose of ethics and morality – is purely functional, they must assure safety and well-being of the majority, and if this inevitably requires sacrificing of the minority, that social ethics always justifies this. Ethics and aesthetics have absolutely nothing in common, although they are frequently confused by human beings.

Sigmund Freud has shocked the puritan society of the early 1900-s saying, that every human being is partly an animal, and human behavior is frequently affected by unconscious animal instincts. He ash also provided detailed description of neurosis mechanism in his work "Civilization and its Discontents".

Most civilized societies impose most of moral and ethical restrictions on an individual, and this, in turn, demands to put harder strain and restrictions on one's animal instincts. Statistics confirms, that most civilized countries have the highest suicide rate.

This repression mechanism becomes automatic, unconscious, and an individual is no longer aware of repressed desires and instincts. Thus, an entire part of person's psyche that is cut off, repressed, out of conscious, but nevertheless, it does cause powerful, but non-direct influence on one's behavior. Carl Gustav Jung called this part of our psyche as "The Shadow". Because the shadow mostly consists of the most basic, primitive, animal parts of ourselves, it is not very pleasant to accept the fact, that those "freaks" are parts of ourselves, especially, if you have received puritan upbringing. And even though, if you may not be a puritan, it is far more pleasant to consider yourself as a completely civilized being without vices, pretending (to yourself in the first place), that this ugly, dark side does not exist at all. It is the same thing as to clean up only a half of a room really well, and pile up all the garbage in the other half, and try to ignore it. Ignoring one's own shadow existence is actually a very convenient hypocrisy. (Sigmund Freud defined this as a "repression defense mechanism"). It also allows to avoid the responsibility for one's own shadow's actions. The shadow is thus perceived as "not me". This is why humans cannot bear any real responsibility for their own actions.

When puritan morality comes into play, and demands even more severe repression of one's own instincts, it makes things much worse. The Third Newton's law says; " Every action causes equal and opposite re-action". When repression of instincts becomes too severe, it inevitably backfires. It's the same thing as to try to drawn a dozen of ping-pong balls in a bath with one hand – they will inevitably slip between your fingers and surface.

The problem is that repressed desire eventually frees itself form the tyranny of morality, and after that it always manifests in some perverse form. One such example –is pedophilia among Catholic priests. This obviously not a recent problem, it has existed for centuries, but it has always been silenced. Sexual desire as such is not evil by itself, but after being so severely repressed, it did find its way out as a perversion. Such cases (and this is probably not the worst example), do stress the necessity to face one's own dark side.

When owned as t host relevant, alive truly whole/holy parts of ourselves, these most basic "dark" energies can be wonderfully demonic, transforming us into vibrant, creative, fully actualized human beings (well, maybe, even into something better, that regular human beings actually). It is only when they are denied, cut-off, repulsed, repressed, that their darkness can become demonic, twisting, exploding destructively into consciousness, swamping ego-rationality in mass psychoses, and in the small daily horrors, that assault us.

—Linda Falorio, *Shadow Tarot*

As it is said "Demon is but an angel, acting out of turn". Some professionally spiritual people are vile and untrustworthy, when off duty, simply because their beliefs conflict with basic drives, and only manage to distort their natural behavior temporarily. The demons than come screaming up out of the cellar at unexpected moments.

—Peter J. Carrol, *Liber Kaos*

Basic principles of demonology:

1. A god ignored is a demon born.
2. That, which is denied, gains power, and seeks strange and unexpected forms of manifestation.
3. Deny death and other forms of suicide will arise.
4. Deny sex and bizarre forms of its expression will torment you.
5. Deny love and absurd sentimentalities will disable you.
6. Deny aggression only to stare eventually at the bloody knife in your shaking hand.
7. Deny honest fear and desire only to create senseless neuroticism and avarice.

Self-hypocrisy, denial of one's negative aspect also exists on a national scale. To be able to make a sober, objective judgment of any particular culture, one needs to take a position of a detached observer – any native representative of that particular culture will always turn a blind eye to its negative aspects.

For example, the occupation of China by Japanese army during the 2-nd World War is still called as "Manchurian Incident" in Japan. Many representatives of Japanese academic elite still consider the "Manchurian Incident" as a proof of superiority of

Japanese nation. I guess, there is no need to mention those atrocities, that were done towards Chinese people (using humans as biologic material to test bacterial weapons, etc.)

But, when Hiroshima is mentioned – crocodile tears are cried, and a lot is said about inhumanity and atrocity. It looks, like humanism and compassion become significant when those, who mention them need to be treated with compassion – in other cases, when such treatment is expected of them – other values become more significant (like the necessity to prove the superiority of one's nation).

Another example – is Moses form the Old Testament. That genocide, that he commenced after entering the Land of Canaan, is in no way different from those atrocities, that Hitler had done

In Nazi Germany. If such comparison seems shocking, than it needs to be reminded, that Hitler also had a status of a messiah, and "Mine Kaumph" was their Holy Bible.

During the 2-nd World War Eastern Orthodox clergy has sent quite a bunch of grateful letters to Hitler, blessing him to lead the "holy war against the Satanic kingdom" (Soviet Union). Nevertheless, the majority of people still firmly believe, that Hitler was the terrible monster, and Moses – was the holy man. One can see Christian cartoons for children about Moses no TV. Can you imagine cartoons about Hitler for kids?

The next example – France shortly after it was relieved from the occupation by Nazi, it has sent its own troops to occupy Vietnam.

Unfortunately, average human beings always turn a blind eye to negative aspects of own culture. And if you do make those negative aspects visible, the reaction that inevitably follows, is quite predictable, and it is ALWAYS very aggressive. Again, this is not a conscious feedback, but a strictly conditioned Pavlovian dog reaction. If you try to explain to an Orthodox Jew the similarity of those atrocities, done by Moses and Hitler – his feedback is in no way going to be friendly.

Another example is that caricature of Mohammed the Prophet in Danish newspaper. It would be interesting to investigate the archives of Middle Eastern newspapers – their caricatures are a lot nastier, for sure, but of course...." your own shit never smells bad".

And it seems strange, that humanistic philosophers still wonder why human beings cannot live in peace, understanding and harmony. If human beings stubbornly refuse to understand themselves in the first place, how can they understand others?

Humanistic philosophy is based on the assumption, that human beings are conscious beings, and they are able to take responsibility for their own actions. This is not true. It is much easier to rely on convenient "solution packages" (holy scriptures, 10 commandments, etc, etc.). There is no need to think of cause- and-effect relations and consider possible outcomes of every particular action in every individual situation.

But this is not possible to create laws that will work perfectly in every situation, lawyers can confirm this – endless corrections and additions in law system are being created all the time.

As an example, let us consider one of the basic Judeo-Christian commandments – "Thou shall not kill". Murder is definitely a sin in a street fight – when only a few people are involved. In a different situation, let's say, during a military conflict between nations, when a few thousand people are involved (instead of only a few people) –that a murder is "a holy duty", and priest from both sides give their blessings for murder. It happens, that the only difference between a "morbid sin" and "a holy duty" is but a scale of a conflict.

Speaking about military conflicts between nations, it needs to be stressed, that resources are becoming scarce, and only in

15 years fresh water is going to be accessible only to 1/3 of human population. Taking these facts into account, one can imagine the upcoming fights for resources between nations (or corporations).

This is why at present time there is a real necessity for spiritual evolution of human beings – the necessity to surpass restrictions, that define human mentality.

To be able to do this, one need to get rid of duality, that is so typical for human psyche, and stop denial of one's dark side. The major obstacles on this path are ethical/aesthetical stereotypes and illusions. A lotus flower, that grows in a swamp amidst mud is a very good metaphor to describe this typical duality of human psyche. Flower's beauty is greatly contrasting with mud, that surrounds it. This metaphor is very much favored by puritan spiritual gurus, that preach absolute transcendence and denial of animal aspects of human psyche.

Somehow, they ignore the fact, that this beautiful flower is only half of the plant. The other half, that is not visible – is not so good looking. This beautiful flower is completely dependent on its dirty and stinky roots – try to cut it off, and it's not going to live for too long. Those parts are absolute opposites of each other absolute polarities, and nevertheless, they are but different parts of the same plant, that are absolutely dependent on each other.

This metaphor actually provides the solution for very sophisticated moral dilemma, and it illustrates the principle of unity and mutual dependency of the opposites. This lotus flower may indeed raise above mud, but this mud is but its food supply. Therefore, these primitive, animal, hideous aspects of our psyche are energy resources, on which our exalted, spiritual side is absolutely reliant.

To illustrate this dependency, we can discuss Indian saint Mahatma Ghandi. He was known for his strict ascetics – absolutely no alcohol, meat, and of course – no sex. Nevertheless, he was known to have enjoyed Platonic company of beautiful women, and he celibately shared his bed with his young niece.

Spiritual fire, burning inside Ghandi, would have become quickly extinguished without that sexual energy exchange (with his own minor niece) – and even though, this energy exchange was a lot less intense, than during physical sex, it was still sex – albeit, in a very subtle form.

Of course, Mahatma Ghandi is a saint for millions of people. Let's take another example: prominent fiction writer Arthur Clark, that was knighted by English Queen Elizabeth the 2-nd, is also the icon for the world's intellectual elite. When Lisa found out, that he has arranged himself a pedophile liar on Ceylon, she immediately stripped him of this title. When I told about this to a great fan of Arthur Clark, who also had Doctor's degree in psychiatry, his reply was : "One cam of course blame a pedophile... but will this make sense? Pedophilia is very difficult to cure...". Even though, he had a Doctor's degree, he didn't dare to question that socially accepted stereotype and authority of Arthur Clark.

Speaking about integration of the shadow side into a human psyche, I would like to stress the importance of the right way of doing it. By no means I reject the necessity of controlling one's animal instincts. But is absolutely necessary to understand the obvious harm and negative consequences of excessive control of one's passions – this is something, that puritan moralists prefer to ignore.

It is absolutely normal and natural, that we are partly primitive and hideous beasts – these animal parts of ourselves use dirt and excrements as the basic energy resource that is later transformed into beautiful flowers of spirituality.

Obviously, one needs to understand the dangers of overdoing it. Using a little excrement as a fertilizer is good, but if you dump an entire truck of fecal on a plant, you are going to bury it. Opposites MUST be carefully balanced by each other. ✦

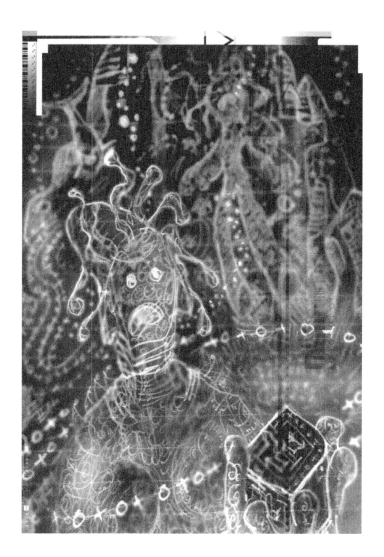

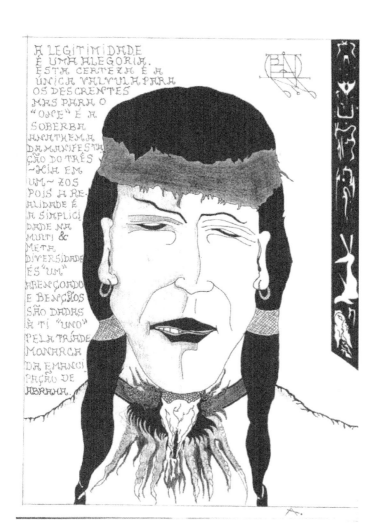

A LEGITIMIDADE
É UMA ALEGORIA.
ESTA CERTEZA É A
ÚNICA VÁLVULA PARA
OS DESCRENTES
MAS PARA O
"OSCE" É A
SOBERBA
ANATHEMA
DA MANIFESTA
ÇÃO DO TRÊS
~XIA EM
UM~ AOS
POIS A RE-
ALIDADE É
A SIMPLICI
DADE NA
MULTI &
META
DIVERSIDADE
ÉS "UM"
ABENÇOADO
E BENÇÃOS
SÃO DADAS
A TI "UNO"
PELA TRÍADE
MONARCA
DA EMANCI
PAÇÃO DE
ABRAHA.

The Zos Kia Cultus
by a Lover of Ecstasy

Claudio Cesar Carvalho

In my point of view the Zos Kia Cultus has a rich and fascinating perspective which must be explored in the depths of the sub-consciousness. It shows how the continuing attraction of irrational can embody imperceptibly on a subtle iconography from sacred Spirit – our Iconoclast – in several ways and possibilities.

Zos Kia Cultus as a Current is a common sense for several people and it is still widely used as a term by occult art's critics, writers, occultists, scholars and even artists. Nevertheless, through my experience and natural surrender to my Arte I perceived about brevity of this term aforementioned as I have been penetrating in psychology of the Void or KIA. My natural linking in past lives to Typhonian Tradition lead me back to a specifically evaluation of what could be this ablaze impulse so-called Zos Kia Cultus.

According to my point of view, Zos Kia is a rich, powerful and still vital language of images and styles in which comes to represent a deep-rooted inner 'systems' from individual as a whole organism sentient encompassing millions ideas and contexts in ΘNE. Thus the individual can liberate intense primal atavisms latent in the depths of your sub-consciousness. Thereby, this powerful impulse can provide a profound disruption of the senses which lies on unwanted emotional and psychological states. These unwanted states are restrictive agents of the persona because they take the benefit of conventional nominalization and mentality so that it can be easily expressed along the cruelty of the barriers of the rational contributing to a stupid personality cult for other people.

To express Zos Kia as a Current and nothing else, it would be exactly the understanding about the Expressionism term like "pathetical ism" abrogating so its own expression and genuine meaning.

Both AOS and Kenneth Grant fully understood, each to his term, which really means Zos-Kia, that is to say, they 'saw' beyond the context of a Current, they saw a vast Impulse. In my viewpoint, in this case, Kenneth Grant worked intensively the irrational pattern that establishes Zos-Kia's emanations as vehicle between the Consciousness and Unconsciousness; however, Austin Spare acted in an intuitive way although he created a model of access from very personal way to reach and establish contact with this Impulse. It's can be understood as a root without form, this means that the individual should not stick to the illusion's fields from the mind, but inversely walking down the road of imagination that is quite different. ✦

Blackmouth Beach

Sean Woodward

SHE slammed the brown bag on the kitchen table with a far off look and an exclamation.

"Drongos!" said Bambrah

"What's the matter love?" I asked, opening the fridge and rearranging the vegetable shelf as she started to pass the contents of the bag. She paused, hands on hips, giving me that 'don't call me love look.'

"Well, I was coming back past the bakery and some idiot in a blacked out ute bombed down the road towards the beach. They could've killed someone the speed they were doing".

"Well, you know what Fossil Beach is like, the tourists can't wait to get down there with a hammer. They all think they'll find the next T-Rex!"

She smiled a little then and passed me the milk.

"It was Ozraptors back home. I've seen that Range Rover before though. Last week parked down Sea Lane. Bunch of preppy kids with clipboards, seemed to be asking people lots of questions."

"Preppy?"

"You know, just out of Uni, not quite learnt a proper fashion sense yet. One of your lot."

"Says you!" I stretched past the fridge door and poked her playfully in the ribs, my blow buffeted by the softness of her hand- knitted, rainbow colored, Nepalese cardigan.

"Anyway'" I said hoping she'd calmed sufficiently. "Did you get the September copy of New Scientist?"

"Yeah, it's in the bag, just make sure you recycle it and don't just add it to that pile in the spare room."

I leant over to the table and pulled the magazine out. Sure enough, it was the issue Tommy had been talking about in the pub. I flicked past the articles on dark energy and black holes, past the usual climate change scares and found it. The Bloop. Some kind of underwater anomaly Tommy had said. Thought I'd be interested. He didn't really see the point of the field recordings I was making around the village and the beach, but was impressed that I'd managed to get the funding to undertake it.

"You're right though about those kids," I said, putting the magazine down after my cursory scan. "I think it's something to do with this article I was telling you about last night. I had an email from Dr Muller this morning, apparently there's a new exchange programme with a University in Massachusetts. He said they might need the expertise of an award-winning sound designer like myself."

"Well, you tell them from me, they need the expertise of a driving instructor first!"

She'd bypassed my part in the human unpacking chain and finished emptying the bag with haste. I wasn't sure if I was the anger driving her or something else.

"Let's go for a walk up to Vicarwood," she said, shutting the fridge door and smiling at me "I've saw some new shrooms while I was out."

I didn't know it that morning but it was the mushrooms that had first stretched then let slip the chains of my sanity. It was hard to fathom now, walking down Blackmouth's beach in the

icy hours of the morning. How could a small circle of mushrooms in a September field mean so much? But I understand it
all now. Watching the distant waves break and seeing their energy dissipated at the shoreline I recognize the same relentless
erosion that tugs at the blowing threads of my mind, without
ceasing, without pity, fingers of wind searching for one to unpick
and utterly dismantle my faculties.

I turn my eyes from the level horizon towards the dark cliffs
of the Jurassic Coast. In the brittle black termite towers of rid-
dled caves and porous edifices I see the homes of the insect serv-
ants, building high their lookouts, in a frenzy of swarming, suf-
focating activity. I know they're waiting for the low pitched sig-
nal from the sea, amplified for them by the sand and the dark
cliffs that they have slowly sculpted into sound mirrors. They're
waiting with twitching limbs for the Deep Hoo Ones to crawl
from the water's edge. I know they wait patiently, hoping a
chance will soon come for them to show their devotion, their
tireless, numb waiting.

I'd heard the rumours of course. All the old fishermen were
full of them, even Mr Johnson who usually was a man of few
words on any other subject. He'd prop his metal detector up
against the sea wall by the car park, take out his favorite scrim-
shaw pipe and by the time he had completed his ritual of scour-
ing, emptying and refilling it with clumps of Golden Virginia to-
bacco his thoughts would settle on the tales of some of the
strange metal objects he'd found. The early morning dog walk-
ers of the village were the same if you managed to wade beyond
the usual half-hearted exchange of "Morning!" With them
you'd also find yourself in the shallows of odd conversations.

In fact, it didn't seem to take much coercion at all for the
locals to offer up some of their own tales of strange happenings
on the shoreline. The same way the salt arrived on the back of

the wind and began to eat at every piece of metal below the tumbling cliffs, so gradually the stories snagged a place in your mind, gathering themselves about a dark, salt-worn spot the longer you exposed yourself to the biting wind by the water's edge. Massing together, the stories would seem plausible and after a while it was easy to forget common sense, easy to act in ways you would never have thought possible, easy to abandon the simple survival reflexes that long ago were saying "run, get out of here now!".

Of course I can't turn from the shore's edge. That would be to admit defeat, to leave Bambrah stranded. Even now I dare not think of all the things she has seen in those depths, all the wet lurking horrors that lie by her side in the waking dreams of the Deep Hoo Ones.

I have to put such thoughts aside, concentrate my purpose on keeping the structure of my mind intact, hang on to the lines of strategy that I hope to enact, wrap myself around the shape of the plan, find some comfort in its hopeful warmth. It's not easy. With each seabird call, each blow of the wind upon my skin, all I can think of is her. Of how different life would be if we'd gone back to Sydney, like she'd always wanted.

"Come on Steve, there's nothing here, let's get some breakfast, eh?"

I looked up, wrenched from my thoughts. Tommy must have been jogging towards me for a good ten minutes. I recognized his gait immediately, he didn't let up his pace, timing his words exactly for the moment that he passed me and headed up the shingle towards the car park and the small waterfront cafe.

"Sure I'll be there in a sec." I said, knowing it would be much longer. As quickly as he'd traversed the beach he was gone, an aerodynamic flash of thermally insulated North Face cladding and Nike propulsion. The furry hood was down on my own jacket. I wanted to feel the elements make my flesh raw. No amount of clothing could insulate me from this place, keep out the memories that blew hard against my face, yet unseen to all others.

I scanned the sands ahead. No more visitors, good. I step over a mooring line, all barnacled and rusted, it's orange-flaked tendrils like a huge plant stem, unfurled by the tide. It looked no different from all the others that stretched out to sea further down the beach.

But this was the one. I could tell from the position of the headland to my side, I didn't need a GPS or the familiar siren of Mr Johnson's metal detector as he wandered the sandy grass behind the beachfront cafe. This was the one Tommy and the others had lined up alongside, had gripped tight though their hands bled, had steadfastly joined as if in some summer tug of war contest. This was the one that my foot had become tangled with in those cold waters, this was the one that had wrenched me from the depths. This was the one that had torn my hand free from hers.

Does screaming really resolve anything? Every morning I come to this spot, to this uncaring line of metal and I want to scream at it until there is no breath left in my lungs. I want to rip it from the beach, tie it round my neck and walk back into the water. At first I tried to do that, to recreate the bond that led me here, to find some solace from the events. But the line was too well anchored, too heavy. By the time I had realized my efforts were in vain something of the urge had passed, worn itself out in the face of insurmountable odds. So when action fail you begin to make plans. Plot in the small hope that you will succeed. I know it's the only way to stop the voices too. If I concentrate on the plan then their gurgling underwater incantations might slowly start to recede.

And what of my plan? I dare not tell Tommy of the things I saw down there. So instead we;d sit in the cafe and he'd orders two full English breakfasts and we'd eat. Him with his cups of tea, me with my coffee, in a large Lily mug. Every morning since that night, the same ritual. He'd watch me over his knife and fork, trying to gauge my state of mind. I could see it in the tilt of his head, the raised eyebrow, the expectant pauses in his eating.

Every morning I'd cut the sausages, butter the toast and move the mushrooms to the side of the plate. Yesterday was the day that Tommy's curiosity finally got the better of him.

"I've noticed you don't touch the mushrooms anymore. You always used to like them." It was half fact, half query. He was trying to be careful, trying not to be too blunt. It was something I liked about Tommy, probably why we'd been friends so long. He had perfected just the right amount of interest, just the right amount of distant British bloke-ness. So yesterday I finally decided maybe there was something I could share with him. I drank some more coffee then put the cup down slowly, carefully.

"They were really Bam's favorites. You know how she
preferred organic "Yeah, sure"
food"
"Well, that was the start of things"
"Things?"
"Well, she grew whatever she could herself, always preferred her own. Hated the supermarket ones. It was one of the reasons we came to Blackmouth, no supermarkets within a fifty-mile radius! She hated the fact that no matter what the labels said you never really know what chemicals they'd been subjected to all the time they were growing. When we first went out together, she had this little book of mushrooms that she took everywhere with her. I-Spy book of mushrooms I think. Anyway, you know Vicarwood? She could name every plant in there. But mushrooms were her thing.

Loved them, would take me on expeditions for hours tracking down the latest ones.

"Yeah, always thought she was a bit of a hippy." Tommy half smiled, not quite sure he should have said that.

"I guess she was" I said, taking some more of the buttered toast from the rack Mrs Johnson had replenished whilst we were talking.

"Well, she found a circle of them up on the headland. Kept going on about how perfectly formed they were, how we had to go up and try them."

"Try them?"

"Well according to her book, and she swore she'd double-checked online, they were the magic variety."

"What did I say Steve, bit of a hippy".

"So I went with her up to the headland. Figured it was safest if there was two of us. That way if she did anything stupid, you know, like jump off the path, I could stop her."

"Did she?"

"What? Do anything stupid. Not then. But yeah, something really stupid"

"What were they like?"

"You mean you've never tried them?"

"Me? C'mon Steve, you know my body is a temple"

"Yeah I can see that by the amount of bacon and eggs it consumes! At first nothing happened. Sure we giggled a lot, lay around in the grass watching the clouds, pretending we could see omens of everlasting love, ships and a million daydream shapes. I think that initial lack of result was what lowered my guard. I figured they weren't so magic after all."

"But it put you off eating any for breakfast?"

I looked around the cafe. As we had been talking, Matherson and Omagh, the other regulars had left, Mrs Johnson was back in the kitchen and the place held just the two of us and the assortment of fishing tackle decoration.

"Look Tommy. I know what you and the other guys think after what happened to us. I know exactly this is going to sound."

"It's ok mate, do you no good to keep it bottled up"

"OK. It started slowly at first. The mushrooms on the headland more and more obsessed Bam. Every time we'd go out for a walk she'd steer our route through Vicarwood and onto the headland. Just in case there were any fresh ones she'd say. And there always were. So we'd eat some. We started seeing things Tommy, hearing things too. It was always at the headland that I would see the shapes in the trees. Well, more than shapes. I saw babies in the knots of the wood, a bark teeming with them! Every tree Tommy! Imagine that, animated writhing babies in the bark. But the voices were worst."

I knew I should have stopped then. Tommy was starting to fidget. "I couldn't quite understand them at first. It was like an old record played slowly or backtracked. There was a strange wetness to it too. It's hard to describe. A dullness. As we ate more of the mushrooms it became clearer. Bam heard it too. We tried to work out what was being said, if we even heard the same thing. We did."

I moved the toast rack and leant over the table, closer to Tommy and whispered "Yohar n'phel Dagon! Yohar da'ath bon"

"What the hell is that supposed to mean?" asked Tommy, pulling back from me and wiping sauce from his chin.

"I don't know, but it had a hypnotic quality, made you want to follow the sound, find out where it was coming from"

"Oh, I think that's fairly obvious!" said Tommy.

"No. We heard the same things Tommy!"

"Well I can understand it putting you off mushrooms! is that why you two ended up in that boat in the middle of the night? Chasing voices out at sea?"

"No" I lied. " she wanted to go skinny dipping".

Tommy laughed "that was Bam all right! Look, I won't tell anyone about this, god knows it's hard enough for you at the moment. If there's anything I can do to help you, you know you can ask don't you?"

"Course I do." I could see he wanted no more of this talk. "Same time tomorrow?"

"Yep, got to keep the body in shape!"

Tommy would probably be wondering where I was by now. Remembering yesterday's conversation had only taken a few minutes but it was enough to make me realize I had to stick to the plan. Maybe Tommy would start to keep more than his body in shape after today. For a moment I thought about the cold, it was enough to make me pull up the hood on my jacket. I looked around the beach one last time. Nobody about. Good. The voices were getting strong again. Amongst them I could hear Bam's voice. Trying to concentrate on hers only I began to walk towards the sea, following the mooring line that had so recently saved me from its depths. With each step my clothes become more waterlogged, heavier. For long moments I can feel the ground beneath my wet shoes and then suddenly it's gone and I'm floating, head barely above the salty waves

They pull me down before I have chance to change my mind. I feel tight hands squeezing their grip on my ankles as the water's surface rushes past my head, past my eyes. I instinctively try to hold my breath, clinging to the ways of the surface dwellers, but it's too late. I can see toad-like hands groping in my pockets, taking the talismans and charms of protection that I had planned to barter with. So easily the Deep Ones deprived me of my weapons. I was foolish to think I could enter their domain alone. I should have found someone who would understand. I should have found someone to sell me a gun.

"Relax" says Bam as they pull me even deeper. The darkness begins to give way to a distant mauve glow below. My captors have let go of me now and I move forwards. I'm left alone as a blur of forms retreat through the murky water. It's like being in a dream, not quite sure of perspective, of colours or speech. There is a twisted, distorted tangent to everything. Finally I feel the seabed beneath my shoes. I walk slowly towards the source of the purple light, aware now that somehow my breathing continues. I pass through the trapezoid dissections of mauve, the very same ones that consumed our boat and see at last a dark city.

I hear her. "Come to me my sweet," says Bam.

Ahead is a bed of purple coral and writhing forms. She sits within a ring of huge bone-like purple mushrooms. My mind feels different, my thoughts have become waterlogged. Images pass before my inner eye as clear as those before me. The fibrous web of the mushrooms reached through the seabed like the gossamer labyrinth of a were-spider that hangs at the gateway between worlds, that reaches across the vast seas of space to colonize another world, to spread the spores of their consciousness between the cold places and abysses of waiting night. They speak to me in their shining cyberlight language, spinning their thoughts in and out of reality. A race of sleeping star travelers, the history of generations encoded in their spores, spun into sub atomic trapezoid structures, bobbing like flotsam on the ocean top. A type of understanding dawns, dulls my horror of seeing Bam before me, her body strangely bloated, her eyes bulging, her back arched by the weight of a scaly spine. As I look my horror turns to a smile, knowing that soon mine too will be that way, that soon we will live amidst wonder and glory in the invisible country. ✦

Become A Living God

Publisher

T HE definitive motto of human transcendence: Become A Living God welcomes magickians to maximize their individuality, freedom, and personal power in this lifetime. Browse a catalog of courses, rituals for hire, physical grimoires, talismans, consultations, and readings at BecomeALivingGod.com.

NOXAZ: VOLUMES 1 & 2
Edgar Kerval, Asenath Mason, Bill Duvendack & more

QLIPHOTH: OPUSES 1, 2, 4, 5 & 6
Edgar Kerval, Asenath Mason, Bill Duvendack & more

COMPENDIUM OF BELIAL, VOLUME 1
E.A. Koetting, Kurtis Joseph, Asenath Mason & Edgar Kerval

COMPENDIUM OF LUCIFER, VOLUME 2
E.A. Koetting, Kurtis Joseph, Edgar Kerval, Bill Duvendack, Asbjörn Torvol & Frank White

THE COMPLETE WORKS OF E.A. KOETTING
E.A. Koetting ✶